E

MW01616041

The Musical

Book and Lyrics by
George Reinblatt

Music by
**Frank Cipolla, Christopher Bond,
Melissa Morris, and George Reinblatt**

Music Supervision by
Frank Cipolla

Additional Lyrics by
Christopher Bond

Additional Music by
Rob Daleman

A SAMUEL FRENCH ACTING EDITION

SAMUEL
FRENCH
FOUNDED 1830
NEW YORK HOLLYWOOD LONDON TORONTO
SAMUELFRENCH.COM

RENTAL MATERIALS

An orchestration consisting of **Piano/Conductor Score, Guitar, Drums, and Music Accompaniment and Underscoring CD for rehearsal and performance** will be loaned two months prior to the production ONLY on the receipt of the Licensing Fee quoted for all performances, the rental fee and a refundable deposit.

Please contact Samuel French for perusal of the music materials as well as a performance license application.

IMPORTANT BILLING AND CREDIT
REQUIREMENTS

All producers of *EVIL DEAD: THE MUSICAL must* give credit to the Author of the Play in all programs distributed in connection with performances of the Play, and in all instances in which the title of the Play appears for the purposes of advertising, publicizing or otherwise exploiting the Play and/or a production. The name of the Author *must* appear on a separate line on which no other name appears, immediately following the title and *must* appear in size of type not less than fifty percent of the size of the title type.

Billing must be substantially as follows:

(NAME OF PRODUCER)

Presents

EVIL DEAD: THE MUSICAL

Book and Lyrics by
George Reinblatt

Music by

Frank Cipolla, Christopher Bond, Melissa Morris, George Reinblatt

Music Supervision by
Frank Cipolla

Additional Lyrics by
Christopher Bond

Additional Music by
Rob Daleman

The required additional billing as follows:

**BY SPECIAL ARRANGEMENT WITH
RENAISSANCE PICTURES, LTD. & STUDIO CANAL IMAGE, S.A**

EVIL DEAD: THE MUSICAL first glimpsed the light of day in Toronto, where early workshop engagements played to capacity and beyond. While mainstream theatre audiences flocked to the show, diehard fans of the *Evil Dead* film series made pilgrimages from across North America to witness the birth of a new cult hit. The popular workshop production enjoyed two sold-out runs at Toronto's Transac Club in 2003 before heading off to Montreal in 2004 as part of the 22nd Just For Laughs Festival.

EVIL DEAD: THE MUSICAL opened in New York Off-Broadway produced by Jenkay LLC, Jeffrey Latimer Entertainment, Just for Laughs Live, at New World Stages on November 1, 2006 to rave reviews from both critics and audiences. The performance was directed by Christopher Bond and Hinton Battle, with sets by David Gallo, costumes by Cynthia Nordstrom, lighting by Jason Lyons, sound design by Peter Fitzgerald and Kevin Lacy, special effects and makeup design by Louis Zakarian, fight choreograhy by B.H. Barry, choreography by Hinton Battle, and sound effects design by Michael Laird. The production stage manager was Jane Pole. The cast was as follows:

LINDA . . . . Jennifer Byrne

CHERYL . . . . Jenna Coker

SHELLY . . . . Renée Klapmeyer

ASH.. . . . . .Ryan Ward

SCOTT. . . . . Brandon Wardell

ED.. . . . . .Tom Walker

ANNIE . . . . Renée Klapmeyer

MOOSE . . . . .Tom Walker

JAKE.. . . . . Darryl Winslow

FAKE SHEMP. . . . . Ryan Williams

SPIRIT OF KNOWBY. . . . . Brandon Wardell

The band consisted of:

CONDUCTOR/KEYBOARDS . . . . Daniel Feyer

GUITAR/BANJO . . . . Jake Schwartz

DRUMS/PERCUSSION . . . . Brad "Gorilla" Carbone

CHARACTERS

ASH – College student, male, baritone.

CHERYL – College student, female, alto.

ANNIE – Mid-twenties, female, alto. (Actor playing **ANNIE** also plays: **SHELLY**)

LINDA – College student, female, soprano.

SCOTT – College student, male, tenor.

ED – Mid-twenties, male, bass. (Actor playing **ED** also plays: **MOOSE**)

JAKE – Mid-thirties, male, baritone.

FAKE SHEMP – Male. This role is basically all of the small roles in the show…the severed hand, the headless body, etc. (NOTE: This role is optional, and if the director desires, these small roles can be divided up amongst the other actors in the show.)

A NOTE ON CASTING

If the director desires the cast to be larger, doubled roles may be expanded into individual parts.

MUSICAL NUMBERS

ACT I

CABIN IN THE WOODS

HOUSEWARES EMPLOYEE

IT WON'T LET US LEAVE

LOOK WHO'S EVIL NOW

WHAT THE FUCK WAS THAT

JOIN US

GOOD OLD RELIABLE JAKE

HOUSEWARES EMPLOYEE (reprise)

I'M NOT A KILLER

ACT II

I'M NOT A KILLER (reprise)

BIT PART DEMON

ALL THE MEN IN MY LIFE KEEP GETTING KILLED BY

CANDARIAN DEMONS

ODE TO AN ACCIDENTAL STABBING

DO THE NECRONOMICON

IT'S TIME

WE WILL NEVER DIE

BLEW THAT BITCH AWAY

ACT ONE

Scene One

(A lone spotlight comes up on a giant Necronomicon at the top of the stage. The book opens on its own, as the text, written in blood, fills the page.)

KNOWBY. *(V.O.)* Legend has it that it was written by the Dark Ones. Necronomicon ex Mortis, roughly translated, "Book of the Dead." The book served as a passageway to the evil worlds beyond. It was written long ago, when the seas ran red with blood. It was this blood that was used to ink the book. In the year thirteen hundred A.D., the book disappeared.

(The book slams shut. Lights up on ASH, LINDA, SCOTT, SHELLY and CHERYL in a car.)

SONG: CABIN IN THE WOODS

ALL.

WE'RE ALL JAMMED IN THE CAR
AND WE'RE GOING REALLY FAR
DRIVING DEEP INTO THE TREES
WITH HOT DOGS, CHIPS, AND CHEESE

TO MAKE THE WEEK GO QUICKER
WE PACKED A TON OF LIQUOR
RYE AND TROPICANA
WE'LL GO TOTALLY **BANANAS**!

SPRING BREAK VACATION IS JUST BLING BLING
CAUSE SOMETHING IN THIS MUSKY AIR MAKES US
    WANT TO SING

ALL. *(cont.)*

>CABIN IN THE WOODS (OOOH)
>A CABIN IN THE WOODS (YEAH)
>WE'RE FIVE COLLEGE STUDENTS ON OUR WAY TO AN
>OLD ABANDONED CABIN IN THE WOODS (OOOH
>YEAH)

(spoken)

ASH. Well kids, after a three hour drive, I can officially say, we're here.

SHELLY. I don't see any cabin in the woods.

ASH. That's because it's in the woods. The woods just up there. But this is as far as the road goes. In order to get to the cabin, we have to cross this footbridge. **(ASH** *points to a small bridge)* It is the only way to the cabin. The only way.

LINDA. Oh Ash, as much as I love working with you everyday at S-Mart, I think this vacation will be even better.

ASH. I couldn't agree more, Linda. Sometimes it's healthy for a boyfriend and girlfriend to leave their place of employment and just have some fun as a couple, in a non S-Mart related setting. **(LINDA** *crosses the bridge.)*

CHERYL. Thanks for bringing me along, Ash.

ASH. Please, Cheryl. Would it be a spring break vacation if I didn't drag along my lonely sister? **(CHERYL** *crosses the bridge.)*

SHELLY. Hey Ash, thanks for letting me come on this trip.

ASH. Well, Shelly, if you were good enough for Scott to pick up drunk in a bar three days ago, then I just know you're good enough for me to spend my only holiday of the year with. **(SHELLY** *crosses the bridge.)*

SCOTT. This cabin deal better get me laid.

ASH. I'm sure it will Scotty. I'm sure it will.

SCOTT. *(to the girls, while crossing bridge)* Hey, wait for me! Shit!

ASH.

ALL MY FRIENDS ARE HERE
FOR THE BEST SPRING BREAK OF THE YEAR
AWAY FROM SCHOOL AND FROM S-MART
FOR A WEEK WAY OFF THE CHARTS

LINDA.

A HOLIDAY WITH ASH
ALL THAT I'D EVER ASK
HE'S SO CUTE AND THIN
AND THAT'S WHY I LOVE HIM

SCOTT.

THIS WILL BE JUST LIKE CAMP
BUT WITH A SLUTTY TRAMP
IN A FEW HOURS YOU WILL SEE ME
DOING THE NASTY IN A TREE

SHELLY.

SCOTT'S LOOKING TO GET BUSY
BUT FRESH AIR MAKES ME DIZZY
I'M SO HIS PERFECT GIRL
OH LOOK, THERE GOES A SQUIRREL!

CHERYL.

A WEEK UP IN THE WOODS OF PURE TRANQUILITY
A CHANCE FOR ME TO REST IN A NICE FACILITY
I CAME UP TO THIS CABIN TO READ AND SLEEP AND
    BAKE

SCOTT.

HOPE OUR HEADBOARD RATTLIN' DON'T KEEP YOUR
    PRUDE ASS AWAKE!

ALL.

CABIN IN THE WOODS (OOOH)
A CABIN IN THE WOODS (YEAH)
WE'RE FIVE COLLEGE STUDENTS ON OUR WAY TO AN
    OLD ABANDONED CABIN IN THE WOODS (OOOH
    YEAH)

(spoken)

LINDA. Hey Ash! What's this place like anyway?

ASH. Well, it's an old place. A little run down, but it's right up in the mountains. And the best part is, we're staying there for free.

LINDA. Yeah, why are we getting this place for free?

CHERYL. What kind of landlord rents cabins for free?

SCOTT. No landlord rents cabins for free. That's why we're not renting it.

LINDA. What?

ASH. Yeah, I forgot to tell you girls. We're not exactly renting this cabin.

SCOTT. We're breaking in.

CHERYL. No!

ASH. Don't worry. No one will find out. At this time of year, the owners won't be there.

SHELLY. You mean, we're breaking into an empty cabin in the woods? I don't like the sounds of this.

SCOTT. What can possibly go wrong with five college students breaking into an abandoned, secluded cabin in the woods, where no one knows where we are?

SHELLY. Well, when you put it that way!

ASH.

     THIS TRIP WILL BE WACKY FUN

LINDA.

     SEVEN DAYS TO SNUGGLE MY HONEY BUN

SHELLY.

     A WEEK OF DRINKING

SCOTT.

     AND PREMARITAL SEX

CHERYL.

     AND TONIGHT I'LL MAKE SOME SNACKS OUT OF
     HERSHEY BARS AND CHEX!

ALL.

> LISTEN TO US NOW AND MAKE NO MISTAKE
> WE'RE GONNA HAVE FUN CAUSE IT'S SPRING BREAK
> WE'LL POUR, WE'LL SCORE, WE'LL FALL FLAT ON THE
> FLOOR.
> WE'LL DO ALL THIS AND A WHOLE LOT MORE – IN
> OUR

> CABIN IN THE WOODS (OOOH)
> A CABIN IN THE WOODS (YEAH)
> WE'RE FIVE COLLEGE STUDENTS ON OUR WAY TO AN
> OLD ABANDONED CABIN IN THE WOODS

ASH & LINDA.

> WE'RE FIVE COLLEGE STUDENTS ON OUR WAY TO AN
> OLD ABANDONED CABIN IN THE WOODS

SCOTT & SHELLY.

> WE'RE FIVE COLLEGE STUDENTS ON OUR WAY TO AN
> OLD ABANDONED CABIN IN THE WOODS

CHERYL.

> WE'RE FIVE COLLEGE STUDENTS ON OUR WAY TO AN
> OLD ABANDONED CABIN IN THE WOODS

ALL.

> CABIN IN THE WOODS

(Exit all.)

Scene Two

(Inside the cabin. The group enters.)

ASH. So this is our cabin in the woods. Isn't it great?

EVIL FORCE. Join Us.

CHERYL. Did you hear something?

SCOTT. No.

(SCOTT runs back to the bedrooms.)

LINDA. Look at this place. Oh, it's fantastic, Ash.

ASH. Sure is, Linda.

SHELLY. Ohhh windows…fancy.

(SCOTT returns.)

SCOTT. Wow. You should see all the bedrooms back there. They're fuckin' awesome. Me and Shelly call the one with the big bed.

SHELLY. Oh Scotty! Good thinking.

SCOTT. Well Shelly, when I'm with you, one of us has to be doing the thinking.

CHERYL. I feel funny about being here. What if the people who own the place come home?

ASH. They're not gonna come back. Even if they do we'll tell them the car broke down or something like that.

LINDA. With your car, they'd believe it.

SCOTT. Stop worrying Cheryl. Why don't you go read or something?

CHERYL. Maybe I will.

(CHERYL pulls out Bruce Campbell's book "If Chins Could Kill.")

SCOTT. *(to SHELLY)* What's her problem?

SHELLY. I know. She thinks she's so smart just 'cause she can read.

ASH. This is the life. All the important people in my life here together. My girlfriend. My sister. My best friend. And of course you Shelly, who I only just met. But still, I couldn't think of four other people in the world I'd rather spend my vacation with. I would very much like to make a toast for all this evening. *(holding up a glass)* As a Greek friend of mine once said, "Oh nis nis tu tu tarine."

LINDA. Which means?

SCOTT. Party down!

(Suddenly, the cellar door flings open on its own.)

ASH. What was that?

LINDA. Whatever it is, it's still down there.

CHERYL. I don't like cellars. Let's just close it up. It's probably just some animal.

SCOTT. An animal? An animal? *(laughs)* That is the stupidest thing I've ever heard of. Jesus Christ. What a stupid bitch.

CHERYL. Well then maybe it was the wind.

SCOTT. The wind? We're inside! I thought what you said before was stupid. But now *that* is the stupidest thing I've ever heard. What a stupid bitch!

LINDA. There's definitely something down there. And it probably is just some animal. Ash, remember when we had that raccoon in the basement at S-Mart?

ASH. Remember? I had to use a broom, a laundry hamper and a Swiffer just to get rid of it. But don't worry loyal S-Mart shoppers, we removed the animal and S-Mart was once again rodent-free.

SCOTT. Well, you guys are probably right. Probably is just some animal. Here Cheryl, why don't you go down 'n check, make sure?

CHERYL. Scotty! I'm not going down there!

SCOTT. Ha ha ha. What a stupid bitch!

ASH. Come on Scott; let's go see what that was.

SCOTT. Okay, okay...this looks like a job for the guy with the big balls.

SHELLY. Be careful.

ASH. Back in a minute.

(SCOTT and ASH climb down into the cellar.)

LINDA. Hey Ash! Scotty! You find anything? Ash. Scotty. Ash! Scott!

SHELLY. They're just kidding around...aren't they?

CHERYL. Guys, stop screwing around. Are you okay? Say something.

LINDA. Ash!

SHELLY. Scotty?

(SCOTT jumps up and scares everyone.)

SCOTT. BOO!! Ha ha ha, you dumb assholes. God-damn what a bunch of pansies.

ASH. Look at all the cool stuff we found. Help me up with it.

SCOTT. *(taking items from ASH)* Check it out. An axe, a gun.

ASH. I bet it still shoots.

SCOTT. Probably does.

(SHELLY holds the barrel up to her face. SCOTT pulls it away.)

SCOTT. Hey do you guys sell these at S-Mart?

(SCOTT holds up a dagger.)

ASH. Ancient daggers? No.

LINDA. What else you got there, Ash?

ASH. Oh God. Look at this book.

(ASH holds up the Necronomicon.)

LINDA. Creepy.

SHELLY. Super creepy!

ASH. It's not even in English.

CHERYL. Guys, we shouldn't be going through this stuff. It's not ours.

SCOTT *(mockingly)* We shouldn't be going through this stuff. It's not ours. Shut your pie hole, Cheryl! Goddamn. You're always ruining our fun. Hey look – a tape recorder. Okay, shhhh…let's see what's on it.

(SCOTT plays the tape recorder.)

KNOWBY. *(on tape)* This is Professor Raymond Knowby, Department of Ancient History, log entry number two. I believe I have made a significant find in the Castle of Candar, having journeyed there with my daughter Annie and Associate Professor Ed Getly. It was in the rear chamber of the castle that we stumbled upon something remarkable; Necronomicon Ex Mortis, roughly translated, the "Book of the Dead." The book is bound in human flesh and inked in human blood. I brought the book to this cabin where I could study it undisturbed. It was here that I began the translations. The book speaks of a spiritual presence; a thing of evil that roams the forests and the dark bowers of man's domain. It is through the recitation of the book's passages that this dark spirit is given license to possess the living. Included here are the phonetic pronunciations of those passages. *Cunda astratta montose eargrets gutt nos veratoos canda amantos canda*

CHERYL. Shut it off!

KNOWBY. *Canda*

CHERYL. Shut it off!

KNOWBY. *Canda*

CHERYL. *(screaming)* Shut it off!!!

(A tree smashes through the window. **CHERYL** *screams and exits to the bedroom.)*

LINDA. Cheryl, don't go! It was just the wind. Scott, how could you?

(**LINDA** *follows* **CHERYL** *into the bedroom.*)

ASH. Scott, why did you keep playing that tape? You saw it was upsetting Cheryl. You just don't know when you're taking something too far.

SCOTT. It's just a joke! Jesus Christ. I was just screwing around.

ASH. Still, you scared her half to death.

SCOTT. So the wind blew a tree through the window. Ohhhh, scary. Geez, no one around here knows how to have any fun. Come on Shelly, lets go scare Cheryl some more by making the windows rattle in our bedroom. And when I say make the windows rattle...I don't mean by some unstable weather pattern...I mean we'll be having sex.

SHELLY. Okay Scotty.

(**SCOTT** *and* **SHELLY** *exit.*)

Scene Three

(LINDA enters.)

ASH. Is Cheryl all right?

LINDA. Yeah, she's fine. She was just a bit freaked out by that tape.

ASH. That's my sister for you, always running scared of old audio recordings.

LINDA. Ash, I know she's been acting up a bit, but it was still very nice of you to invite your sister up this week.

ASH. Honey, you talked me into it.

LINDA. I know, but still. It was very considerate of you. You're a kind and sweet and generous person, and Cheryl's lucky to have you.

ASH. Listen; let's forget about Cheryl. We're here in this cabin. Alone. This should be time for us.

LINDA. You're right. It is pretty romantic up here.

ASH. What do you say we have some champagne, huh baby? After all, I'm a man and you're a woman... least last time I checked.

LINDA. Okay.

ASH. I have something else for you too.

(ASH gives LINDA a jewelry box. LINDA opens it to reveal a necklace.)

ASH. So what do you think kid?

LINDA. Oh Ash, I love it. Would you put it on?

ASH. Oh yeah, sure. I was going to give it to you before we came up here, but things got so hectic, this is really the first chance we've had to be alone.

LINDA. Oh Ash! It's beautiful. I really love it. I promise I'll never take it off for as long as I live. Who ever thought when I took that job at S-Mart that I would meet the man of my dreams?

ASH. Well, I never thought I'd fall in love with one of my co-workers either. Nothing about that in the S-Mart employee manual.

SONG: HOUSEWARES EMPLOYEE

ASH.

LITTLE DID I KNOW THAT DAY
WHEN I DROPPED OFF MY RESUME
AT THE LOCAL S-MART STORE
THAT ANOTHER EMPLOYEE I'D FALL FOR

LINDA.

MY JOB WAS IN THE CHECKOUT AISLE
S-MART SERVICE WITH A SMILE
I HATED WORK, IT WAS A BORE
BUT ALL THAT CHANGED WHEN YOU WALKED
    THROUGH THE DOOR

ASH.

I WAS ASSIGNED TO AISLE THREE.

LINDA.

AND THAT IS WHERE YOU FELL FOR ME.

ASH.

A LOVE SO STRONG IT HAD TO BE

LINDA.

PERFECT RETAIL...

ASH & LINDA.

HARMONY
I HAVE TO ASK A QUESTION TO THE GODS ABOVE.
HOW WERE WE DEEMED WORTHY OF THIS PERFECT
    LOVE?
I'LL ASK THE TREES, I'LL ASK THE SKY
I'LL ASK THE WHOLE WIDE WORLD

ASH.

HOW DID A HOUSEWARES EMPLOYEE LAND THE
    PERFECT GIRL?

LINDA.

> HOW DID THE PERFECT GIRL LAND A HOUSEWARES
> EMPLOYEE?
> I COULD BARELY FOCUS ON MY CHECKOUT LINE
> YOUR POLYESTER SHIRT ALWAYS ON MY MIND
> FANTASIES TOOK OVER ME
> I'D FORGET TO SCAN ITEMS AND GIVE 'EM FOR FREE

ASH.

> HOW COULD I CONCENTRATE ON HOUSEWARES?
> WHO CARES ABOUT BLENDERS WHEN YOU'RE RIGHT
> THERE
> OUR ROLES REVERSED THERE IS NO DOUBT
> CAUSE I WAS THE ONE WHO WAS CHECKING YOU OUT

LINDA.

> I HAD A MAJOR CRUSH ON YOU

ASH.

> WHEN I WAS NEAR YOU MY LOVE GREW

LINDA.

> FINDING LOVE AT WORK, IT MUST HAVE BEEN FATE

ASH.

> IT'S BETTER THAN MEETING ON ELIMIDATE.

ASH & LINDA.

> I HAVE TO ASK A QUESTION TO THE GODS ABOVE.
> HOW WERE WE DEEMED WORTHY OF THIS PERFECT
> LOVE?
> I'LL ASK THE TREES, I'LL ASK THE SKY
> I'LL ASK THE WHOLE WIDE WORLD

ASH.

> HOW DID A HOUSEWARES EMPLOYEE LAND THE
> PERFECT GIRL?

LINDA.

> HOW DID THE PERFECT GIRL LAND A HOUSEWARES
> EMPLOYEE?

ASH.

> STOCKING THE SHELVES
> WAS ALL I THOUGHT WOULD BE
> BUT FINDING MY TRUE LOVE AT S-MART
> THAT MAKES THIS JOB SO GROOVY

LINDA.

> I HAVE TO ASK A QUESTION

ASH & LINDA.

> TO THE GODS ABOVE.
> HOW WERE WE DEEMED WORTHY OF THIS PERFECT
>   LOVE?
> I'LL ASK THE TREES, I'LL ASK THE SKY
> I'LL ASK THE WHOLE WIDE WORLD

ASH.

> HOW DID A HOUSEWARES EMPLOYEE LAND THE
>   PERFECT GIRL?

LINDA.

> HOW DID THE PERFECT GIRL LAND A...

ASH & LINDA.

> HOUSEWARES EMPLOYEE?

ASH. *(spoken)* Gimme some sugar baby.

> (**ASH** *and* **LINDA** *kiss and exit together.* **CHERYL**
> *enters, passes the couple, and heads towards the*
> *kitchen.)*

Scene Four

EVIL FORCE. Join Us! Join Us!

   (**CHERYL** *pops her head up from behind the counter.*)

EVIL FORCE. Join Us! Join Us!

CHERYL. Hello?

EVIL FORCE. *(in as normal a voice as possible)* Join us!

   (**CHERYL** *knows the sound is coming from outside. She starts to head for the door, and pauses.*)

CHERYL. Now mother always said that whenever you hear a strange, frightening, and potentially life-threatening ghostly chant coming from the dark woods that there's only one thing you should do... not wake the others and go investigate it alone!

   (**CHERYL** *exits.*)

   (*Outside the cabin.* **CHERYL** *is walking through the trees [well, 3 people dressed as trees]. Every time she turns her back, the trees move behind her.*)

CHERYL. Hello? Is anybody out here? All I see are these trees.

EVIL FORCE. Join Us.

CHERYL. Hello.

EVIL FORCE. Join Us.

CHERYL. I heard you. I heard you before.

EVIL FORCE. Join us!

CHERYL. I know someone is out here.

EVIL FORCE. Join Us.

   (**CHERYL** *is attacked by the trees.*)

   (*blackout*)

Scene Five

(Inside the cabin. ASH, LINDA, SCOTT *and* SHELLY
are eating brownies. CHERYL *bangs on the door
from outside.)*

CHERYL. *(offstage)* Ashley! Open the door! Ashley!
Ashley!

(ASH opens the door. CHERYL *enters, beaten and
bruised, with her clothes ripped to shreds.)*

ASH. Cheryl?

SCOTT. What the hell happened to you?

ASH. Are you okay?

LINDA. What's wrong?

SHELLY. Her name's Cheryl right?

ASH. Cheryl, did something in the woods do this to
you?

CHERYL. No! It was the woods themselves! They're
alive, Ashley! The trees! They're alive.

LINDA. Ash, why don't I take her in the back room so
she can lie down.

CHERYL. I'm not lying down! I want to get out of here.
I want to leave this place right now. Right now
Ashley!

SCOTT. Wait a minute. I sure as hell ain't leaving any
place tonight.

SHELLY. Cheryl.

LINDA. Cheryl.

SCOTT. Come on Cheryl; is now really the time to be
acting like a stupid bitch?

ASH. Cheryl, there's nothing out there. Trees do not
attack people.

CHERYL. Ashley! Will you drive me into town or not?

ASH. What? Right now? Look, sure, sure, I'll take you
into town, but just listen to what you're saying.

CHERYL. I don't care how it sounds. I wanna get out of this place right now.

ASH. Okay, maybe you could stay somewhere in town tonight. Come on let's go to the car.

(SCOTT and SHELLY groan in protest.)

ASH. Don't worry everyone, I'll get her in a motel and be back in no time. Our vacation will resume as planned momentarily.

LINDA. This is very sweet of you Ash. When you get back, I'll bake you some cookies.

ASH. Sounds like a plan. Come on Cheryl.

(ASH and CHERYL exit. As the lights begin to fade, SCOTT motions to LINDA and SHELLY for a ménage-a-trois.)

LINDA. No.

(blackout)

(Outside the cabin. ASH and CHERYL are walking through the forest.)

ASH. Don't worry; you'll be in a safe hotel in no time. And maybe then you can calm down, purchase a film on Spectravision, raid the mini-bar, steal as many little soaps and shoe horns you can fit in your bag...

CHERYL. You believe me, don't you Ashley? You believe that there's something out here.

ASH. Well it doesn't matter if I believe you. I'll take you to town, and leave it at that. We just have to cross this bridge...

(The lights come up on the bridge, covered in caution tape.)

CHERYL. The bridge!

ASH. How did this happen? It's been destroyed. There's no way out of here.

SONG: IT WON'T LET US LEAVE

CHERYL. CAN'T YOU SEE?
WHY DON'T YOU BELIEVE?
IT WON'T LET US LEAVE,
IT WON'T LET US LEAVE.

LISTEN TO ME
WHY DO YOUR EYES DECEIVE?
FINALLY BELIEVE
IT WON'T LET US LEAVE,
IT WON'T LET US LEAVE.

*(**ASH** hugs **CHERYL**.)*

(blackout)

Scene Six

(The airport.)

AIRPORT ANNOUNCER. *(V.O.)* Flight 86A the hourly shuttle from Cairo has just landed in Terminal One. Once again, that's Flight 86A, the *hourly* shuttle from Cairo. Terminal One.

(ANNIE enters carrying luggage. ED is waiting for her.)

ANNIE. Ed!

ED. Annie! How was –

ANNIE. How was my flight? Not great. Spiderman was the in-flight movie. And yeesh! Let's just say that was poorly directed. But let me tell you about my expedition. I found the missing pages from the Book of the Dead.

ED. What condi –

ANNIE. What condition are they in? Take a look. They haven't aged a day in over three thousand years. Maybe longer.

ED. When do –

ANNIE. When do we begin the translations? Tonight. I hope everything is all set with my father. I haven't spoken with him in a week. There's no phone in the cabin. We'll take your car; it'll take us about an hour to get there.

ED. You hinted –

ANNIE. Yes. I did hint in my telegram that my father was on to something in the first part of his translations.

ED. What –

ANNIE. What was it he found in the Book of the Dead? Probably nothing. But just possibly, a doorway to another world.

ED. There –

ANNIE. Thanks for pointing that out Ed. There does appear to be a slight tear in my sleeve.

ED. You –

ANNIE. You're right. We can fix it when we get to the cabin.

ED. I –

ANNIE. Oh, I missed you too, Ed.

ED. G –

ANNIE. No, *I'm* glad we finally had this chance to talk.

(**ANNIE** *and* **ED** *exit.*)

Scene Seven

(Nighttime, in the cabin.)

(ASH is playing the tape recorder by himself in the corner. CHERYL is looking out the window with her back to the audience. LINDA is just sitting there.)

KNOWBY. *(on tape)* It's only been a few hours since I've translated and spoken aloud the first of the demon resurrection passages from the Book of the Dead. May God forgive me for what I have unleashed unto this earth. I have seen the dark shadows moving in the woods and I have no doubt that whatever I have resurrected through this book is sure to come calling...for me.

LINDA. Ash honey, why don't you stop playing around with that tape. Why don't we play a game.

ASH. In a little bit, baby.

LINDA. Okay. Scott, Shelly, you guys wanna play a game?

SCOTT *(offstage)* Coming.

(SCOTT enters zipping up his fly. SHELLY follows wiping her chin.)

SCOTT. What are we playing?

LINDA. Let's play Guess the Word.

SHELLY. How do you play that?

LINDA. Well, I'll give you some clues and you try to guess the word.

(SHELLY looks confused. LINDA pulls out a stack of game cards.)

LINDA. Okay, first word. It's big. It's green. It goes in the water.

SHELLY. Toaster.

LINDA. Close. Ummm...Blank *Dundee.* It rhymes with rockodile. Starts with a "C."

SHELLY. Coaster.

LINDA. No. No, the word was Crocodile. Okay next card. It's when you're playing football and you score it's a –

SHELLY. A rouge!

CHERYL. *(still with her back to the group)* A touchdown.

LINDA. Right, Cheryl. Okay when you eat lunch on a blanket in a park it's a...

CHERYL. Picnic.

LINDA. Okay when I go –

CHERYL. Butcher.

LINDA. Right. Okay it's a –

CHERYL. Vitamin C.

(They all look at each other strangely. **LINDA** *goes through the cards quickly.)*

CHERYL. *(continuing)* Muscle, porridge, dental floss, quintuplets, hamster.

SCOTT. She's been studying the cards. Nobody's that good at Guess the Word.

LINDA. Cheryl, is everything okay?

(horn hits [from this point on, every time someone turns into a demon, the same opening horn hits from "Look Who's Evil Now" will play])

(CHERYL *turns and reveals she is a demon.)*

SONG: LOOK WHO'S EVIL NOW

CHERYL.

WHY HAVE YOU DISTURBED OUR SLEEP?
AWAKENED US FROM OUR ANCIENT SLUMBER
YOU WILL DIE! NIGHTMARE IS BEFORE YOU.
LIKE OTHERS BEFORE YOU, YOU'RE GONNA TUMBLE.

CHERYL. *(cont.)*

> ONE BY ONE
> WE'RE GONNA TAKE YOU.
> ONE BY ONE
> NOTHING YOU CAN DO
> ONE BY ONE
> YOU'LL SURELY FALL
> ONE BY ONE
> WE'RE GONNA KILL YOU ALL.
>
> NOW I'LL ASK YOU A QUESTION, NOT WHERE OR WHY
>   OR HOW!
> BUT **WHO**?
> LOOK WHO'S EVIL NOW!

*(**CHERYL** collapses on the floor.)*

SCOTT. What the hell happened to her? I mean I've seen games of Guess the Word bring out the worst in people, but that's fucking ridiculous.

ASH. Guys, I think that when we played that tape, some evil force must have been awakened that took over Cheryl's soul and made her a demon.

SCOTT. Thanks for the update, C.S.I. Miami. I think the rest of us figured that one out already.

LINDA. Did you see her eyes? Oh Ash, I'm scared. What's wrong with her?

ASH. I'm no doctor, but she looks sick. Let's put a blanket on her.

*(**ASH** puts the blanket on **CHERYL** and just like James Brown she hops up and throws the blanket off.)*

CHERYL.

> WHOOAAAAAAAAA!!! SOCK IT TO ME, BABY!
> LOOK WHO'S EVIL
> LOOK WHO'S EVIL
> LOOK WHO'S EVIL NOW

CHERYL. *(cont.)*

> I SAID A LOOK WHO'S EVIL
> LOOK WHO'S EVIL
> LOOK WHO'S EVIL NOW
>
> I HEARD YOU SUCKERS MOCKING ME AND CALLING ME
>   A PRUDE
> LETS SEE IF YOU'RE STILL LAUGHING WHEN I RIP OUT
>   YOUR FALLOPIAN TUBES
> I'LL TWIST YOUR FUNBAGS AND BEAT YOUR BROWN
>   EYE BLUE
> THEN I'LL SMASH YOUR SACK AND MAKE A TESTICLE
>   FONDUE
> JUST TRY AND FUCK WITH ME
> I'LL SHOW YOU WHERE YOUR GRAVE IS
> IF BEING EVIL'S COOL
> CONSIDER ME MILES DAVIS
> NOW I'LL ASK YOU A QUESTION, NOT WHERE OR WHY
>   OR HOW
> BUT **WHO?**
> LOOK WHO'S EVIL NOW!

(spoken) Now I told you earlier I would take you all out one by one, and I'm not one to make false promises, so kids, let's kick it!

> FIRST ASH,
> I'LL WHOOP YOUR ASS
> THEN SCOTT,
> I'LL BUST YOUR NUT
> THEN SHELLY,
> I'LL SLASH YOUR BELLY
> THEN LINDA,
> I'LL STICK A PENCIL IN YA!

(CHERYL *stabs* **LINDA** *in the ankle with a pencil.)*

(spoken)

LINDA. My ankle! I can't walk.

ASH. Take her to the bedroom and make sure she's okay.

CHERYL.

> YOU CAN'T STOP ME
> YOU CAN'T STOP ME
> YOU CAN'T STOP ME NOW

> I SAY YOU CAN'T STOP ME
> YOU CAN'T STOP ME
> YOU CAN'T STOP ME NOW

> *(SCOTT and ASH grab CHERYL and throw her in the cellar. They lock it up with a chain, but there is enough slack so that she can still pop her head out.)*

CHERYL. You didn't stop me. You didn't stop me. You just delayed me momentarily. Who's the stupid bitch now Scotty? Who's the stupid bitch now?

> *(They slam the cellar door shut.)*

SCOTT. This is freaking me out, Ash.

ASH. Me too, buddy. Me too. I mean my sister just turned into a demon.

SCOTT. And a pretty fuckin' foul mouthed demon as well. Are we gonna be okay Ash?

CHERYL. *(popping up)* Dead by dawn. You'll all be dead by dawn!

> *(CHERYL closes cellar door.)*

ASH. Uh. Yeah Scotty. We're gonna be fine. Perfectly fine. Well, we will be fine just as long as no one else in our party turns into a demon.

SHELLY. *(screams from the bedroom)* Ahhhhhhhh!

ASH. Fuck!

> *(horn hits)*

> *(SHELLY enters, a demon.)*

SHELLY. Look who's evil now!!!

SCOTT. Not Shelly too!

SHELLY.

> OH MY GOD LIKE LOOK AT ME AND MY EVIL DEMON
> BOD
> NOW WATCH ME SHOVE THIS HIGH HEEL STRAIGHT
> UP YOUR LOVE ROD
> I'LL TEAR YOUR BODY INTO SHREDS, AND BEAT YOU
> WITH HIS BALLS
> THEN I'LL SWALLOW UP YOUR SOUL WITHOUT
> GAGGIN' AT ALL
> I'M SEXY
> I'M CUTE
> AND SO EVIL TO BOOT
> I'D KILL YOU WITH THESE GUNS, BUT I DON'T THINK
> THEY SHOOT
>
> NOW I'LL ASK YOU A QUESTION

CHERYL. *(spoken)* Sing it!

SHELLY.

> NOT WHERE OR WHY OR HOW
> BUT **WHO?**
> LOOK WHO'S EVIL NOW!
>
> *(spoken)*
>
> Now Scott, since you were so kind as to take me on
> this trip, I've graciously decided that you're going
> to be the first one I will take with me!

CHERYL. Do your thing girl!

SHELLY & CHERYL.

> Join us
> Join us
> Join us
> Join us

SCOTT. Dude, grab the fucking gun! Shoot her! Shoot
it!

> *(As* **SHELLY** *gets closer and closer to* **SCOTT**, **ASH**
> *picks up the gun from the corner.)*

ASH. I can't shoot Shelly. She's a friend of ours.

SCOTT. Goddammit Ash, I picked up that skank drunk in a bar three days ago...

(*ASH throws the gun to* **SCOTT**. **SCOTT** *shoots* **SHELLY,** *sending her flying out the cabin door.*)

SONG: WHAT THE FUCK WAS THAT

ASH & SCOTT.

WHAT THE FUCK WAS THAT?

SCOTT.

YOUR SISTER HAS TURNED INTO A ZOMBIE.

ASH & SCOTT.

WHAT THE FUCK WAS THAT?

ASH.

YOUR GIRLFRIEND WAS A DEMON TOO.

ASH & SCOTT.

WHAT THE FUCK WAS THAT?

SCOTT.

SHE JUST RIPPED MY PRE-RIPPED ABERCROMBIE

ASH & SCOTT.

WHAT THE FUCK WAS THAT?

ASH.

I GOT SOME SHELLY ON MY SHOE.

ASH & SCOTT.

WHAT DARKNESS LURKS BEYOND THIS WOODEN SANCTUM?

WHAT THE FUCK WAS THAT?

SCOTT.

DUDE, THESE HOES BEEN ZOMBIFIED!

I CANNOT STAY HERE ANYMORE. I'M GETTING OUT OF HERE.

ASH.

NO, WE CANNOT LEAVE, LINDA'S ANKLE WON'T MAKE IT I FEAR.

SCOTT.

I CANNOT STAY – I KILLED MY LAY! I MUST GO NOW!

ASH.

YOU CAN'T GO NOW!

SCOTT.

I MUST!

ASH.

YOU CAN'T!

SCOTT.

I MUST!

ASH.

YOU CAN'T!

SCOTT.

BITCHES OUT FOR BLOOD – I CAN'T TAKE THIS
    ANYMORE.

ASH.

WE DON'T EVEN KNOW IF THERE'S A WAY BACK,
EXCEPT FOR THAT DAMN BROKEN FOOTBRIDGE!

JUST LISTEN TO ME.
LINDA CAN'T WALK.
CANNOT HIKE.
CAN'T EVEN STAND!

SCOTT.

GOTTA GO!!
RIGHT NOW!
I'LL FIND A ROAD
WHERE I'LL FLAG DOWN A VAN!
NO I WON'T!
IT'S TIME TO GO!
THEN WE'LL LEAVE HER, THAT'S OUR BRAND NEW
    PLAN!!

ASH & SCOTT.

WHAT THE FUCK WAS THAT?

SCOTT.

NOW I'LL PUT AN END TO THIS VACATION.

ASH & SCOTT.

WHAT THE FUCK WAS THAT?

ASH.

SCOTT DON'T LEAVE ME ALL ALONE

ASH & SCOTT.

NECRONOMICON. THE BOOK OF THE DEAD.

ASH.

THE CHANT –

SCOTT.

A CURSE –

ASH.

THE CHICKS –

SCOTT.

I'M GONE!

ASH & SCOTT.

WHAT THE FUCK WAS THAT?

IT'S THE EVIL DEAD!

(**SCOTT** *exits, slamming door.*)

Scene Eight

CHERYL. *(popping up)* I can't believe you let him walk out on you like that...Scott free.

ASH. Shut up Cheryl.

CHERYL. Where's he rushing to? I guess he's *Scott's* to go.

ASH. Shut up!

CHERYL. That Scott sure made like a tree...and left.

ASH. Stop it.

CHERYL. I was looking forward to biting into his flesh. The commercials say Scott's is the softest tissue.

ASH. Oh come on, that's awful.

CHERYL. I'm awful? You're awful Ash. Look what you've done. You just killed a girl. You locked your own sister in the cellar. Your girlfriend is so hurt she can't even walk. Your best friend just abandoned you. And you, Ashley. Look at you. You're going mad.

ASH. I'm not going mad. I'm not. I'm not going mad!

CHERYL. Why don't you just accept your fate and join us Ashley. Join us!

SONG: JOIN US

CHERYL.

DON'T YOU WANNA JOIN THE CREW?
YOU'LL BE DEAD AND EVIL TOO
THE COOLEST THING TO DO
IS JOIN US

YOUR LIFE SUCKS YOU KNOW,
WORKING S-MART'S GOTTA BLOW
DON'T BE JUST A FUCKIN' SCHMO
AND JOIN US

YOU'LL BE DEAD WITH NO REMORSE
AND BE HUNG LIKE A HORSE

CHERYL. *(cont.)*

> YOU CAN EVEN BANG A CORPSE
> IF YOU JOIN US
>
> IMAGINE ALL THE FUN
> IF TO EVIL YOU SUCCUMB
> SO JUST LAY DOWN THAT BIG GUN

> *(Satanically spoken)* and join our dark army of evil Candarian Demons as we conquer this land, and take over each and every soul of the living!

ASH. No. No. I'm not going to join you. Never!

CHERYL. What's the problem Ash? Don't you want to look beautiful like me!

ASH. Beautiful like you? Please. I'd rather look like this moose!

> *(ASH points to the MOOSE HEAD on the wall. Then, all of the sudden, the MOOSE HEAD springs to life, and bites his hand.)*

MOOSE. Why thank you!!

ASH. The dead moose!

MOOSE. *(laughing)* Actually I'm a Candarian Demon Moose, and I'm here to tell you about all the fun and excitement you'll experience if you take us up on our offer and join us!

> *(sings)*
>
> CAN'T YOU SEE WE'LL HAVE A SCREAM
> EVIL'S FUNNER THAN IT SEEMS
> YOU'LL PLAY ON OUR SOFTBALL TEAM
> IF YOU JOIN US

> *(Suddenly, all of the cabin; the pictures, the books, the fridge…pretty well everything on the set – comes to life and moves with the music. They move whenever the HOUSE SPIRITS have a line.)*

HOUSE SPIRITS. *(coming to life)*

> JOIN US!

MOOSE.

> WE'LL ALL HAVE A BALL
> ORGANIZE A BIG PUB CRAWL
> AND SPEND SUNDAYS AT THE MALL
> IF YOU JOIN US

HOUSE SPIRITS. *(coming to life)*

> JOIN US!

CHERYL.

> YOU CAN SPEAK OUR EVIL SLANG
> EVEN GROW SOME EVIL FANGS
> YOU'LL SCORE SOME EVIL TANG
> IF YOU JOIN US

MOOSE.

> BEING EVIL IS DIVINE
> YOU'LL BE DEAD BUT SO REFINED
> PARTY LIKE IT'S NINETY NINE

> *(Satanically spoken)* If you join our dark forces as we enslave all mankind, chew on their tiny brains and bathe in their hot bubbling blood!!!

ASH. AAHH! All of you shut up! Especially you, Moose. Shut up!

CHERYL. Someone hasn't been watching the Discovery Channel. Everyone knows once Moose get singing, they never shut up.

MOOSE. We never shut up.

ASH. That's it! I'm getting Linda and we are getting out of this place!

> *(All of the doors and windows in the cabin slam shut)*

CHERYL & MOOSE.

> YOU CAN TRY AND TAKE A STAND
> BUT WE HAVE GOT YOUR HAND

ASH. *(spoken)* What are you talking about?

CHERYL & MOOSE.

> IT'S NOT QUITE WHAT WE PLANNED
> BUT NOW WE'VE GOT YOUR HAND.

ASH. *(spoken)* Why do you keep saying that?

CHERYL & MOOSE.

> WE'VE GOT YOUR HAND,
> YES IT'S TRUE WE'VE GOT YOUR HAND,
> YES WE FINALLY GOT YOUR HAND
> TO JOIN US

> *(The stuffed* **BEAVER** *on the counter springs to life.)*

BEAVER. Ha ha!

ASH. What? You've got my hand to join you? No you don't, you bastards. Why do you keep saying you got my hand to join you, huh? Why do you keep saying that?

> *(***ASH*** *looks to his hand that was bitten by the* **MOOSE** *earlier. And much to* **ASH***'s surprise, his own hand turns evil and strangles him.)*

CHERYL. *(childishly)* We've got your hand! We've got your hand!

ASH. You bastards! You dirty bastards! Give me back my hand! Give me back my haaaaand!!

> *(***ASH*** *and his hand get into an elaborate fight. The contents of the cabin start moving non-stop. After a long battle,* **ASH** *leads his hand to the kitchen where he grabs a chainsaw.)*

ASH. Who's laughing now, eh? Who's laughing now?

> *(***ASH*** *uses his mouth to pull the cord and start the chainsaw. He takes the chainsaw to his own hand as blood gushes into his face.)*

> *(blackout)*

Scene Nine

(The woods. ANNIE *and* ED *are walking, lost.* JAKE *is just standing there.)*

ANNIE. It should be right around here, Ed.

ED. Mayb –

ANNIE. You're right. Maybe we should ask for directions. *(to* JAKE*)* Excuse me. Excuse me, strange man wandering through the woods alone. Is this the road to the Knowby cabin?

JAKE. Firstly I wasn't supposed to be wandering these woods alone. I was supposed to be with my lovely wife Bobbie Jo. But I figured what with that Cheryl girl getting attacked by the trees and all; Bobbie Jo would have appeared a bit useless and redundant.

ANNIE. What did you say?

JAKE. Nothing.

ANNIE. Well getting back on topic, is this the road to the Knowby cabin?

JAKE. That's right. And you ain't going there. *(to* ED*)* You neither.

ED. *(giving up without a fight)* Okay –

ANNIE. And why not?

(JAKE *lights a match, which ridiculously lights the other half of the stage, revealing the destroyed bridge.)*

JAKE. The bridge is out.

ED. *(quitting)* Seems –

ANNIE. Ed's right. There must be another way in. There's got to be another road or something.

JAKE. Sure as hell ain't no road. *(to* ED*)* Why the hell do you want to go up there for anyway? Huh?

ED. *(about to tell him)* Well –

ANNIE. That's none of your business.

JAKE. Hey! I just remembered. Why, yeah…that's right. There is a trail. You could follow me. But it'll cost ya.

ANNIE. How much?

JAKE. Forty fi- Hundred buck.

(ED *makes for his wallet to gladly pay.*)

ED. Here –

ANNIE. You're right Ed. How do we know if this guy's even reliable?

JAKE. *(to* ED*)* Reliable! Why you no good city-slicking, over-cologned, v-neck sweater-wearing son of a gun, with your flappin' lips and pompous-ass attitude! How do you know if I'm reliable?

SONG: GOOD OLD RELIABLE JAKE

JAKE.

WHO'S THE WORLD'S MOST RELIABLE HUMAN BEING?
WHO'S THE ONE FOLKS CALL FOR HELP WITH
EVERYTHING?
WHO'S THE ONE MAN YOU CAN COUNT ON WHEN
YOUR LIFE IS AT STAKE?
IT'S GOOD OLD RELIABLE JAKE

WHO CAN HELP YOU WHEN YOU'VE LOST YOUR KEYS?
OR WHEN YOU NEED DOUBLE BYPASS SURGERY?
WHO CAN BE YOUR PARTNER IN A TWO-MAN LUGE?
AND WHO CAN SNEAK A DEAD HOOKER OUT YOUR
HOTEL ROOM?

WHO'S EVERY SENIOR CITIZEN'S FAVOURITE MIME?
AND WHO CAN PASS COURVOISIER LIKE BUSTA
RHYMEZ?
WHO WAS THE INSPIRATION FOR THE SHAMROCK
SHAKE?
IT'S GOOD OLD RELIABLE JAKE

WHO INVENTED THE FORMULA FOR CRAZY GLUE?
AND WHO'S NAILED ALL THE CHICKS ON THE VIEW?

JAKE. *(cont.)*

> WHO WAS THE LAST MAN TO WALK ON THE MOON?
> AND WHO WON THEIR FOURTH OSCAR FOR
>   DIRECTING PLATOON?
>
> WHO'S THE POINT GUARD FOR THE MEMPHIS
>   GRIZZLES?
> AND WHO COINED THE PHRASE "FOR SHIZZLE MY
>   NIZZLE"?
> IT WAS ME CAN'T YOU SEE, I AIN'T NO FAKE
> I'M GOOD OLD RELIABLE JAKE
>
> *(to* **ANNIE.***)* DO YOU BELIEVE I CAN GET YOU DOWN
>   THE PATH?

ANNIE.

> I BELIEVE

JAKE.

> *(to* **ED.***)* AND DO YOU BELIEVE I CAN GET YOU TO THE
>   CABIN?

ANNIE *(running in front of* **ED***)*

> I BELIEVE

JAKE.

> YOU NEED A GUIDE TO GET YOU THROUGH THEM
>   WOODS
> AND I KNOW THAT TRAIL AND I KNOWS IT GOOD.
> YOU CAN TRUST IN ME THERE'S NO MISTAKE
> I'M GOOD OLD RELIABLE JAKE
>
> YOU CAN TRUST IN ME THERE'S NO MISTAKE
> I'M GOOD OLD RELIABLE JAKE

ANNIE. Really Ed? After all that, you still don't think he's reliable?

JAKE. Goddammit!!! Now you no good city slickers follow me. I'll take you to that dang cabin.

> *(blackout)*

Scene Ten

(We return to the cabin to find ASH duct-taping his stub. His severed hand is on the mantle.)

ASH. Hand, we've had some good times together. I never thought it would end like this.

(ASH turns away. As soon as his back is turned, the hand pops up and runs across the countertop. ASH turns back thinking something is different but can't figure out what it is.)

ASH. Like I was saying hand, you got me through more Friday nights than I'd ever like to admit.

(The hand gives a masturbation movement...and this time ASH sees it.)

ASH. Damn you hand!

(ASH tries to hit the hand and instead painfully bangs his stump. The hand runs off.)

CHERYL. *(popping up)* You're tougher than I thought Ash. Gotta *hand* it to you brother.

ASH. Shut up.

CHERYL. Let's hear it for the boy. Let's give the boy a *hand*

ASH. Stop it.

CHERYL. What's your favourite animal at the zoo? The *handa* bear?

ASH. Enough!

CHERYL. Okay, then...who's your favourite cast member on *Who's the Boss*? Tony Hand-za?

ASH. Tony Hand-za. That doesn't even make sense!

(ASH jumps on the cellar door, closing it. SCOTT barges in the cabin door bloodied.)

SCOTT. Ash! Ash!

ASH. Oh my God!

SCOTT. Help me!

ASH. Scotty.

SCOTT. Dude, where's your hand?

ASH. Don't worry about it. Scotty! You're going to be okay. You're going to be just fine. You'll see. What happened to you?

SCOTT. Ash. It's not going to let us leave. We're all going to die here!

ASH. No, we're not going to die.

SCOTT. We're all going to die. All of us!

ASH. No, we're not going to die! We're gonna get out of here. Now, the sun will be up in a few hours or so and we can all get out of here together. You, me, Linda, Shelly. Hmm...well...not Shelly, you shot her through the door. Now listen to me Scotty. Is there a way around the bridge? Scotty! Listen to me please for God's Sake! Scott!! Is there a way around the bridge?

SCOTT. There's a way. A trail. But the trees, Ash. They know. Don't you see Ash? They're alive! It won't let us leave. Ash...death is a bitch. A stupid bitch!

(SCOTT dies.)

ASH. Scotty. Scott! NOOOO!

CHERYL. *(popping up)* Ash, in all that commotion, it looks like I accidentally scratched your favorite Ray Parker Jr. album!

ASH. NOOOOOOO!

(CHERYL closes cellar door)

MOOSE. *(springing to life)* And by the way Ash. I wasn't going to mention it earlier, but your pants look like they have a pretty nasty mustard stain on them. And if I know mustard stains like I think I do, that ain't coming out.

ASH. NOOOOOOOOO! What else can go wrong today?

(horn hits)

(LINDA enters, a demon.)

LINDA. Look who's evil now!

ASH. NOOOOOO!

CHERYL. *(popping up)* We've got your girlfriend! We've got your girlfriend!

ASH. Shut up will you? Shut up! *(in disbelief)* No, not you Linda. Linda. Linda!

> *(ASH shakes LINDA. It doesn't faze her. LINDA starts laughing maniacally.)*

ASH. Linda, come back. Come back.

> *(SCOTT springs back to life and hops to his feet. A few of his guts are sticking out of his stomach.)*

SCOTT. Ash! Kill her! Kill her dude! She's fuckin' evil.

> *(SCOTT dies again.)*

CHERYL. Kill her if you can, loverboy.

ASH. Now, forgive me Linda. I guess I gotta do what I gotta do.

> *(ASH draws the gun on possessed LINDA and she returns to normal.)*

LINDA. Please don't Ash. I'm fine now.

SONG: HOUSEWARES EMPLOYEE *(reprise)*

LINDA.

I HAVE TO ASK A QUESTION TO THE GODS ABOVE

ASH.

HOW CAN THIS BE REAL?

LINDA.

HOW WERE WE DEEMED WORTHY OF THIS PERFECT LOVE?

I'LL ASK THE TREES. I'LL ASK THE SKY. I'LL ASK THE WHOLE WIDE WORLD

ASH.

A LOVE SO TRUE AND PURE
A LOVE TO LAST FOR SURE

LINDA.

> HOW DID A HOUSEWARES EMPLOYEE LAND THE
> PERFECT GIRL?

LINDA & ASH.

> HOW DID THE PERFECT GIRL LAND A HOUSEWARES
> EMPLOYEE

ASH. I love you, Linda.

LINDA. Please, Ash…please don't hurt me. You swore –
you swore that we'd always be together. I love you.

ASH. No, I won't. I won't. I promise. I love you, too,
Linda.

(From beneath the closed cellar door, we hear
CHERYL'S *normal, non-demon voice…)*

CHERYL. Ashley. Ashley, help me. I'm all right now,
Ashley.

ASH. Cheryl?

CHERYL. Unlock this chain and let me out.

ASH. Cheryl?

> *(**SCOTT** springs back to life with even more guts
> hanging out of him.)*

SCOTT. Don't do it dude. She's still a demon. Both of
those bitches are. *(noticing his guts)* Shit.

> *(**SCOTT** dies again.)*

ASH. Sorry, Scotty. That is still my sister down there.
I'm afraid I'm going to have to ignore your dying
wish and open that cellar door.

> *(As **ASH** approaches the cellar, the possessed **CHERYL**
> pops up and tries to grab him but misses.)*

SCOTT. *(springing back to life)* DUDE! I TOLD YOU SO!
(looking at more guts) Fuck. *(dies again)*

CHERYL. *(mockingly)* I'm all right now Ashley! Come
unlock this chain and let me out! Ha ha ha! Dumb
ass! *(**CHERYL** closes cellar door)*

ASH. Ah you bastards! Why are you torturing me like this? Why?

(horn hits)

(LINDA *is once again... a demon.*)

LINDA. Look who's still evil now!

ASH. Nooo!

(LINDA *jumps on* **ASH***'s back, attacking him.)*

LINDA. We're going to get you. We're going to get you. Not another peep. Time to go to sleep. We-ah ha ha ha ha ha ha!

*(***ASH*** *drags possessed* **LINDA** *into the kitchen. A blind in the kitchen comes down so that the audience can only see the actors in silhouette. In the silhouette,* **LINDA** *is replaced by a mannequin.* **ASH** *grabs the axe, and holds it up to her.)*

LINDA. Your lover is mine and now she burns in Hell!

SCOTT. *(jumps up again)* Dude! Chop off her head. And this time fuckin' listen to me cause I'm really fuckin' dying. *(dies again)*

ASH. I'm sorry Linda, I've got to do this. I've got to chop off your head.

LINDA. We're gonna get you. We're gonna –

*(***ASH*** *chops off her head. He exits the kitchen holding a mannequin version of* **LINDA***'s head in one hand, the necklace in the other.)*

ASH. I gotta admit Linda, this isn't the type of head I was expecting from you this weekend *(hanging her necklace on the wall)* I guess you won't be needing this anymore.

LINDA. Not much need for a necklace when you don't have a neck.

ASH. You're still alive?

LINDA. Alive and biting!

ASH. My hand. You're biting my only good hand. Owww! I said for you to die already. Don't make me axe you again.

(ASH wrestles with the head biting his hand. Finally he puts it on the countertop, where LINDA's real head replaces the mannequin head.)

ASH. You're going down. Chainsaw.

LINDA. Useless. It's useless.

(LINDA's headless body [a large guy who looks nothing like her] runs in with the chainsaw.)

LINDA. My body will get you. My body! I always told you I had a killer body.

(The body chases ASH with the chainsaw. ASH jumps over SCOTT – the body tries to follow, but trips on SCOTT and falls to the ground.)

ASH. Now it's time to die, you old hag.

LINDA. You found me beautiful once.

ASH. Honey, you got real ugly.

(ASH shoots the body, killing it.)

(ASH turns his attention to LINDA's head [which is still very much alive]).

SONG: I'M NOT A KILLER

ASH.

I'M NOT A KILLER
I'M AN S-MART EMPLOYEE
AND TO KILL A CO-WORKER
IS AGAINST COMPANY POLICY

BUT YOU TRIED TO KILL ME
SO NOW I MUST SAY GOODBYE
I'M SORRY LINDA
BUT NOW YOU MUST DIE.

(ASH takes the chainsaw to her head as he sings. Blood spatters everywhere.)

DIE DIE DIE DIE DIE DIE DIE DIE DIE DIE DIE DIE
OH, DIE. OH, DIE.
(ANNIE, ED *and* **JAKE** *enter.)*

ANNIE. Daddy, I'm home.

ASH. This isn't as bad as it looks.

(curtain)

End of Act One

ACT TWO

Scene One

(In a scene identical to the previous one, ASH is chopping LINDA's head with the chainsaw. But unlike the end of the last act, LINDA's real head is replaced by a mannequin head and the bodies in the corner are not there anymore.)

SONG: I'M NOT A KILLER (reprise)

ASH.

DIE DIE DIE DIE DIE DIE DIE DIE DIE DIE DIE DIE
OH DIE, OH DIE

(ANNIE, ED and JAKE enter.)

ANNIE. Daddy, I'm home.

ASH. This isn't as bad as it looks.

JAKE. How in the fuck could this not be as bad as it looks?

ASH. Well sure, there's one bloody dismembered head. But at least there's not a huge pile of bodies in the corner anymore.

ANNIE. Oh my God! Where is my father?

(ED goes for ASH.)

ED. What did –

(ANNIE cuts him off and lunges at ASH instead.)

ANNIE. What did you do to him? Where the hell is he? Oh, and now you've ripped my shirt sleeve. *(ANNIE rips off a part of her sleeve.)* You heathen. *(to JAKE.)* Get this murderous bastard out of my father's cabin!

JAKE. Will do.

ASH. Wait a minute, Chief. Let's talk about this.

(**JAKE** *knocks out* **ASH** *with one punch.*)

ASH. *(half unconscious)* Wait. Please don't. The trees. Wait. Please. The trees.

ANNIE. I hope you rot out there.

(*They throw* **ASH** *out the door and put a chain on it.*)

ANNIE. Daddy? Daddy? Oh my god. Daddy? My father isn't here. But these are his things. Where can he be?

(**ANNIE** *plays the tape.*)

KNOWBY. *(on tape)* It's only been a few hours since I've translated and spoken aloud the first of the demon resurrection passages from the Book of the Dead.

ANNIE. *(to* **ED***)* Shhh...Listen up. This is my father's voice.

KNOWBY. *(on tape)* Now I fear that Candarian Demons have overtaken these grounds. May God forgive me for what I have unleashed unto this earth.

ANNIE. Candarian demons?

ASH. Wahhhhhhhhhh!

(**ASH** *slams on the window trying to get back in. Tree branches are visibly hitting him.*)

JAKE. What the hell is that?

ANNIE. Something's out there with him!

ASH. Ah! Ah! Let me in! The trees! They're alive! The trees are alive!

JAKE. The trees are alive!

ANNIE. Well of course the trees are alive Jake, they are autotrophic organisms. But this is no time for a science lesson...

(The branches keep pounding **ASH** *in the face.)*

ASH. Let me in. Help me please!

ANNIE. Let him in.

JAKE. It's a trick, I know it!

ANNIE. Let him in.

> *(***ANNIE*** opens the door,* **ASH** *runs in, wrestles with the trees a bit more, and shuts the door behind him.)*

ASH. *(out of breath)* All right, no one goes out that door tonight. Also, whatever you do, don't go near the cellar.

ED. The cella –

> *(***ED*** walks over to the cellar door.* **CHERYL** *pops up and bites him.* **ED** *falls in pain.)*

CHERYL. I'll get you Ash. I'm like a literal Hulk Hogan. I'll get you brother!

ASH. Shut up!

CHERYL. We're like that Columbia House Ten CDs for a Penny Club. Sooner or later you'll join us!

ASH. Shut up!

CHERYL. I'm like Dom Deluise at an all you can eat fish house – I'll swallow your soul.

ASH. Shut up!

CHERYL. It'll be like you were killed by some guy whose first name happens to be Don – you'll be Dead by Dawn!!!!

ASH. That's it!

> *(***ASH*** slams the cellar door shut again.)*

JAKE. What in the good goddamn is going on around here?

ASH. It's an old tale. You've probably heard it a hundred times. Boy and his friends go on a week long vacation in the woods. Three friends turn into Candarian demons. One friend is killed by a forest

ASH. *(cont.)* of evil trees. Two demons are killed by their boyfriends respectively, while one stays in the cellar trying to kill everything in sight. Like I said, pretty standard stuff.

ANNIE. And do all these demons only speak in bad puns?

ASH. No, as far as I can tell she's the only one who does that.

ANNIE. Yet she's the only one you let live?

ASH. Yeah – sorry about that.

ANNIE. *(overly dramatic)* The question now is...how do we stop this?

ASH. I have no idea.

JAKE. Well that's goddamn great.

ANNIE. My father would know how to stop it.

ASH. Well honey, your daddy ain't here. So the only thing we can do is stay put and ride this out 'til dawn.

JAKE. That's a shitty idea. I ain't staying in this shitty shithole 'til morning. I'm going. I'm going to get on that there trail –

ASH. Nobody's going out that door, not till daylight.

JAKE. Now you listen to me –

ASH. No, you listen to me.

JAKE. No, if one of us is going to be doing the listening...it's you...listening to me.

ASH. No, no, no! When it comes to listening...

Scene Two

(horn hits)

(ED *hops to his feet, a demon.)*

ED. Look who's –

ANNIE. Oh my god – Look who's evil now!

ED. Fuck!

JAKE. Goddammit! Run for your lives.

(ANNIE and JAKE scream and run for the door.)

ANNIE. Ash, run.

ASH. I don't think so.

ANNIE. You're not scared?

ASH. Not at all. You see, whenever you encounter a flock of deadites, you have to realize there is a hierarchy about the whole thing.

ED. Grrrrr!

ASH. Simmer down there, buddy. There's the big time demons who pose a serious threat and then there's what I like to call 'bit part demons'.

ANNIE. 'Bit part demons'?

ASH. Yes, yes. Bonafide extras. Nothing special about them. They pretty much wait around for you to kill them. They'd never kill a guy like me...the main man...the hero, if you will. It's just not how these stories tend to go. And that's who you are buddy, a bit part demon. So excuse me for not being scared.

CHERYL. *(popping up)* And I'm not one to agree with the living. But Ash is right. You are a bit player in this whole thing. You'd never kill a guy like him. Never.

(CHERYL *closes cellar door.)*

ASH. Right. You see?

ANNIE. That's not fair. He's not a bit part demon.

ASH. Come on. He hasn't even spoken more than three words all night. We don't even know his name.

ANNIE. His name is –

ED. It's Ed. Well, Evil Ed now. And you don't have to defend me Annie – they're right. They're completely right…

SONG: BIT PART DEMON

(As the song begins, the lights come down and a lone spotlight illuminates on **ED.** *But the spotlight's placement is just a bit off so that the light is barely missing* **ED***'s face)*

ED.

I'M THAT GUY YOU SEE
IN EVERY HORROR FLICK,

*(***ED*** notices he is out of the light, and dejectedly moves over so that he can finally be seen)*

YOU WOULDN'T REMEMBER ME
I COME AND GO TOO QUICK.

YOU WOULDN'T KNOW MY NAME
I HARDLY EVER SPEAK A LINE;
IF THE HERO KILLS A HUNDRED DEMONS,
I'D BE THE FORGETTABLE NUMBER THIRTY NINE.

CAUSE I'M A BIT PART DEMON
A SMALL TIME MISFIT;
I SAY YOU'LL BE DEAD BY DAWN;
BUT I DON'T REALLY MEAN IT.

I'M A THREAT TO NO ONE,
THE OTHER DEADITES MAKE FUN
OF ME –
EVIL EDDY,
THE BIT PART DEMON.

ANNIE. *(spoken)* But don't you see, Ed. We've been listening to you talk for the past two minutes. You've said a whole lot just now…just you. You're not a bit part demon anymore. You're a lead player. A star.

ED. *(spoken)* You're right! *(sings)*
NOW I SEE
THAT THIS TREND HAS BEEN DISRUPTED
I'VE SAID MORE THAN FIVE WORDS
WITHOUT BEING INTERRUPTED

I'M A BIT PART NO MORE
MY CHARACTER'S HAD A SWING
NOW IT'S TIME FOR THIS DEMON
TO SING, SING, SING

*(Out of nowhere, **ED** grabs a top hat and cane.)*
I…..

*(Before he can rock out – **ED** is shot dead by **ASH**. He falls on the side of the stage and remains there for the rest of the show.)*

ASH. Now you'll have a bit part in hell.

Scene Three

ANNIE. Ed! Oh Ed! Ed! *(wailing)* ED!

ASH. Are you *still* mourning over that half-wit? Get over it, woman.

ANNIE. My boyfriend just died three seconds ago.

ASH. I know. It's time to move on with your life. That's why –

ANNIE. But he was –

ASH. Hey, don't interrupt me.

ANNIE. But he –

ASH. I said don't interrupt me. Listen baby, I'm not some preppy boy toy monkey boy you can just push around, see. I killed that guy already.

ANNIE. How can you be so heartless? So bad?

ASH. Good...bad...I'm the guy with the gun.

ANNIE. I still don't know what you're even doing here in this cabin!

ASH. I could ask you the same question.

ANNIE. It's my family's cabin.

ASH. Did I ask?

ANNIE. Are all men from Michigan such loud-mouthed braggarts?

ASH. Nope. Just me baby...Just me.

(JAKE *is ignoring this argument, staring out the window.*)

JAKE. That's funny.

ASH. What?

JAKE. That trail we came in here on. It just ain't there no more. It's like the woods just swallowed her up.

ASH. How many times do I have to tell you? Those woods have a mind of their own. They're evil. That's why we can't go out there. Not 'til dawn.

ANNIE. Listen to him, Jake.

JAKE. What the…you mean you believe this psycho and his hoo ha jibber jabber?

ANNIE. Sure, he might have broken into my property, killed my boyfriend, and possibly killed my father…but for some reason, I trust him.

JAKE. *(under his breath)* Oh for fuck's sake!

(SFX: Crickets.)

ANNIE. It's so quiet.

(SFX: Loud, crazy sounds.)

JAKE. What in the blue hell was that?

ASH. Maybe something trying to force its way into our world.

ANNIE. That's exactly what I think every time I hear a weird noise.

JAKE. It came from over there.

ASH. We'll all go together.

JAKE. Hell no, you're the curious one.

(ASH heads toward the noise.)

ANNIE. Hey. I'll go with you.

(ANNIE joins ASH. JAKE follows behind, not wanting to be alone. They look around and see nothing.)

JAKE. Shit, I told you there weren't nothing out there no how.

(All of the sudden, the SPIRIT OF KNOWBY appears. [Of course this spirit is really just a guy with a flashlight under his chin.])

JAKE. Holy Mother o' Mercy. It's a ghost.

ANNIE. It's my dad.

ASH. It's a ghost dad!

ANNIE. Daddy!

SPIRIT OF KNOWBY. Annie. There is a dark spirit here that wants to destroy you. Your salvation lies there. In the pages of the book. Recite the passages. Dispel the evil. Save my soul. And your own lives!

(The SPIRIT OF KNOWBY *disappears.)*

Scene Four

ASH. That was weird.

ANNIE. My father…he's…he's dead.

ASH. Yeah, sure seems that way.

ANNIE. He's dead. Gone. He's…he's…I can't believe this is happening again. I just can't believe this is happening again.

ASH. What's happening again?

ANNIE. Well if you insist on prying. Lately, I've been noticing somewhat of a trend in my life, and every time I think it's about to go away, it creeps in again.

ASH. What could possibly be wrong?

ANNIE. Well, all the men in my life keep getting killed by Candarian demons.

ASH. What was that?

ANNIE. I said…

SONG: ALL THE MEN IN MY LIFE KEEP GET-TING KILLED BY CANDARIAN DEMONS

ANNIE.

ALL THE MEN IN MY LIFE
KEEP GETTING KILLED BY CANDARIAN DEMONS.

ASH. *(spoken)* All the men in your life keep getting killed by Candarian demons?

ANNIE.

FIRST THERE WAS ED
A REALLY NICE GUY
DIDN'T TALK TOO MUCH
BUT I DIDN'T MIND

I WAS ALL SET
TO MARRY HIM
BUT BEFORE WE COULD CONSUMMATE
ED WAS KILLED
BY A CANDARIAN DEMON

ASH & JAKE.

> CANDARIAN DEMON, CANDARIAN DEMON, CANDARIAN
> DEMON

ANNIE.

> THEN IT WAS DADDY

ASH & JAKE.

> DADDY

ANNIE.

> WHO I COULD COUNT ON

ASH & JAKE.

> AH-OOO

ANNIE.

> HE LOVED TO READ THE NECRONOMICON

ASH & JAKE.

> BOOK OF THE DEAD

ANNIE.

> HE ALSO ENJOYED

ASH & JAKE.

> AH-OOO

ANNIE.

> PLAYING BOARD GAMES

ASH & JAKE.

> GOOD FAMILY FUN

ANNIE.

> BUT HE CAN'T SINK MY BATTLESHIP NOW
> CAUSE DAD WAS KILLED
> BY A CANDARIAN DEMON

ASH & JAKE.

> CANDARIAN DEMON, CANDARIAN DEMON, CANDARIAN
> DEMON

ANNIE.

> THEY SAY LOVE IS CRUEL,
> AND I BELIEVE THEM
> MY HEART'S ALWAYS BROH-HOHO-KEN
> CAUSE THE MEN IN MY LIFE
> KEEP GETTING KILLED BY CANDARIAN DEMONS

(spoken)

ANNIE. Why?

JAKE. I don't know.

ASH. Annie, baby I know it seems bad now. It always does. But I think you're exaggerating a touch, sugar bee. I mean sure your father and fiancé were killed by Candarian Demons, but that's only two men, isn't it? I mean there's no way that ALL of the men in your life could have been killed by Candarian demons.

ANNIE. Oh no? *(sings)*

> IT WAS HIGH SCHOOL

ASH & JAKE.

> HIGH SCHOOL

ANNIE.

> SENIOR PROM

ASH & JAKE.

> OH YEAH

ANNIE.

> GOING WITH MY STEADY
> HOWIE BRAHM

ASH & JAKE.

> HOWIE BRAHM

ANNIE.

> A PERFECT NIGHT

ASH & JAKE.

> HOWIE BRAHM?

ANNIE.

> LIKE I ALWAYS DREAMED

ASH & JAKE.

> LITTLE GIRL'S DREAM

ANNIE.

> BUT WHEN *STAIRWAY TO HEAVEN* BEGAN
> HOWE WAS KILLED BY

ASH & JAKE.

DAMN

ANNIE.

A CANDARIAN DEMON

ASH & JAKE.

CANDARIAN DEMON, CANDARIAN DEMON, CANDARIAN
DEMON

ANNIE.

ALL MY COLLEGE BOYFRIENDS, AND MY ONE-NIGHT
STANDS
MY MALE CO-WORKERS, AND PLATONIC GAY FRIENDS
EVERY DATE I GO ON ENDS IN DEMON BLOODSHED
AND NOW THAT I'VE MET YOU TWO GUYS, I KNOW
YOU'LL SOON BE DEAD

ASH & JAKE. *(spoken)* What the fuck?

ANNIE.

THEY SAY LOVE IS CRUEL,
AND I BELIEVE THEM
MY HEART'S ALWAYS BROH-HOHO-KEN
CAUSE THE MEN IN MY LIFE
AND I MEAN ALL THE MEN IN MY LIFE
EVERY SINGLE MAN IN MY LIFE
KEEPS GETTING KILLED
BY CANDARIAN DEMONS.

ASH & JAKE.

CANDARIAN DEMONS

Scene Five

ANNIE. Don't you think it's a bit inappropriate to be touching me "there" right now?

ASH. Baby, I ain't touching nothing.

(**ASH** *holds up his hand.* **ANNIE** *looks to* **JAKE.** *He holds up his hands to show her it's not him.* **ANNIE** *turns to reveal that the severed hand is grabbing her ass.*)

ASH. Goddammit, my hand again.

(**ASH** *grabs the hand and tosses it. It appears on the ledge, gives the finger, and runs off.*)

ANNIE. Eww. Gross. Who knows where that hand has been?

ASH. Well, luckily, I do know where that hand has been…but it's still pretty gross.

JAKE. That's it! I'm getting outta here. And with all this weird shit going on, I ain't going alone; you two are coming with me.

ASH. If you're talking about going back out in those woods you can forget it. You heard the ghost. Annie's got to translate those passages.

JAKE. Goddammit.

ANNIE. Okay, as far as I can decipher there are two separate passages. One to manifest the evil forces in the flesh, and another to transport them through a rift in time and space.

ASH. It sure is lucky you not only showed up with these pages imperative for our survival, but that you also know the lost language required to translate them as well.

ANNIE. Well Ash, if it's any consolation, I think we're pretty lucky you're here to shoot things for us. I guess together we make a pretty good –

(With every word, ASH *and* ANNIE *inch closer and closer to each other. But before they get too close...* JAKE *shoots the gun in the air.)*

JAKE. That's right, lovebirds! I'm running the show now. And guess what? We're going to go out there in them woods and head home. And I told you I wasn't going alone.

ASH. You idiot. Those woods mutilated my sister, killed my best friend, and with your own eyes you saw them brutally attack me. Why do you keep insisting on going out there?

JAKE. I got no time for your common sense. We're getting the hell out of here, all of us.

ANNIE. Don't you understand? With these pages, at least we have a chance.

JAKE. Bunch of mumbo jumbo bullshit. These pages don't mean squat.

*(*JAKE *grabs the pages from* ANNIE *and throws them in the cellar.)*

ANNIE. Now that was just stupid.

JAKE. Besides, now you city slickers ain't got no choice. Now move! Move.

ASH. Look. You're nuts.

JAKE. I said move!

ANNIE. No, you stupid fool.

JAKE. I'll blow your fucking head off. I'm your leader now.

ASH. Well hello Mr. Fancy Pants. I got news for you pal; you ain't leadin' but two things right now. Jack and shit...and Jack left town.

JAKE. Oh really?

*(*JAKE *hits* ASH *with the butt of the gun, knocking him to the floor.)*

ANNIE. Now what did you do that for?

(ANNIE *grabs* JAKE, *he shoves her away.*)

ANNIE. And look, now I have another rip in my outfit.

(ANNIE *rips more of her outfit off.*)

JAKE. Boo hoo. Guess you and this jackass will just have to go down to Old Navy and buy yourself a new one.

(*horn hits*)

(ASH *pops up, a demon.*)

ASH. Look who's evil now!

JAKE. Shit!

(ASH *grabs* JAKE *and drags him outside.* ANNIE *puts the chain on the door.* ASH *reaches through the door trying to grab her, but he can't break though the extremely weak door chain.*)

ASH. Join us!

(ANNIE *slams the door on him. The door begins to slam open, but the chain is preventing it from opening fully. It is unclear who is slamming open the door.*)

ANNIE. You wont get me, Ash! You'll never get me, Ash!

(ANNIE *sees the dagger, picks it up, unlocks the chain, and stabs through the open door.*)

ANNIE. Take that…

(JAKE *walks in the door with a dagger in his stomach. As it turns out,* ANNIE *accidentally stabbed him.*)

SONG: ODE TO AN ACCIDENTAL STABBING

JAKE.

GODDAMN YOU WOMAN
YOU FUCKING STABBED ME
GODDAMN YOU WOMAN
DO I LOOK LIKE A FUCKING ZOMBIE?

ANNIE.

> IT WAS A MISTAKE
> WHAT CAN I DO TO PROVE I AM SORRY?

JAKE.

> WELL, IN THE FUTURE I'D APPRECIATE IT IF YOU
>   COULD
> *(yelling)* Not fucking stab me!
>
> *(sings)*
>
> GODDAMN YOU WOMAN
> YOU'VE REALLY GOT ME PISSED
> GODDAMN YOU WOMAN
> THIS HURTS LIKE A SON OF A BITCH

ANNIE.

> I DIDN'T MEAN TO HURT YOU
> OR MAKE YOU BLEED
> I'LL MAKE YOU FEEL BETTER
> WOULD YOU LIKE SOME PEPCID A.C.?

JAKE.

> WOMAN LOOK WHAT YOU'VE DONE
> I'M BLEEDING ALL OVER THE FUCKING ROOM

ANNIE.

> THEN TAKE THIS CLOTH *(ripping off a big piece of her
>   clothing)*
> AND APPLY PRESSURE TO YOUR WOUND

JAKE.

> BITCH, GET ME SOMEWHERE SAFE
> THAT THING'S STILL OUT THERE IN THEM TREES

ANNIE.

> NO ONE CAN HURT YOU HERE
>
> *(ANNIE leads JAKE to the other side of the cabin,
> and puts him down right beside the cellar door)*

CHERYL.

> *(popping out of cellar)* WELL, NO ONE BUT ME!
> *(talking)* Come here big boy!

JAKE.

GODDAMN YOU WOMAN!

(JAKE is dragged into the cellar. The cellar door slams for the big finish of this number.)

ANNIE. Jake…

(The cellar door flies open, and blood shoots out of it, completely covering ANNIE. The cellar slams shut again.)

(Evil ASH bursts back into the cabin.)

ANNIE. Please Ash – no! Please. No.

(ASH stalks towards ANNIE, but before he can get to her, a very small spotlight illuminates on Linda's necklace on the wall. ASH is drawn to it.)

SONG: HOUSEWARES EMPLOYEE *(piano reprise)*

(ASH returns to his original human state.)

ASH. *(weeping)* Oh, Linda!

(ANNIE picks up the axe and swings it at ASH, barely missing.)

ASH. No! No wait! Listen to me! I'm all right now. That thing is gone!

(She swings again, barely missing. ASH grabs the axe from her.)

ASH. Dammit! I said I was all right! Are you listening to me? Do you hear what I'm saying? I'm alright! I'm alright. Seeing my girlfriend's necklace made me alright.

ANNIE. But your girlfriend wore that necklace and she was still a Candarian demon.

ASH. I know, it seems a touch inconsistent. But trust me. I'm alright.

ANNIE. Okay, maybe you are. But for how long? If we're going to beat this thing, we need those pages.

Scene Six

(The cellar swings open. **CHERYL** *pops up...holding the pages.)*

CHERYL. These pages? You need these pages? I'll kill you before you ever get your hands on them. I'll kill you Ash. I'll kill you.

ASH. Cheryl. I'm getting sick of you trying to kill me. *(***ASH** *picks up the gun)* See this? This is my boomstick! It's a twelve gauge double barreled Remington, S-Mart's top-of-the-line. You can find this in the sporting goods department. That's right – this sweet baby was made in Grand Rapids Michigan. Retails for about a hundred and nine ninety five. It's got a walnut stock, cobalt blue steel and a hair trigger. That's right. Shop Smart. Shop S-mart. Ya got that?!

CHERYL. I'll swallow your soul.

ASH. Swallow this.

*(***ASH** *shoots* **CHERYL** *and she crumbles. But* **CHERYL***'s hand, still clutching the pages, remains sticking out of the cellar.* **ASH** *pulls the pages from her hand, kicks her lifeless body into the cellar, and slams the cellar door shut, as triumphant music swells.)*

Scene Seven

(ANNIE tries to run to him, but as she tries to move, her skirt gets stuck in the door.)

ANNIE. My skirt is stuck. Oh screw it.

(She forces herself through; ripping a ridiculous portion of her clothing and miraculously leaving her in a perfectly-cut, very-revealing outfit)

(They go in for the kiss...but **ANNIE** *hesitates)*

ANNIE. Are you sure this appropriate? I mean my boyfriend just died twenty minutes ago. And your girlfriend died only about ten minutes before that.

ASH. We can't grieve forever.

ANNIE. You're right.

(They go in for a kiss, but again, **ANNIE** *pulls back.)*

ANNIE. Ash, wait. I think it's time we read the passages from the pages I found.

ASH. Of course.

(In his disappointment, **ASH** *phallically un-cocks his gun to the sound of a slide whistle.)*

ASH. *(continuing)* Dispel this evil once and for all.

ANNIE. Okay, there are two separate passages. Recitation of the first passage will make the dark spirit manifest itself in the flesh.

ASH. Why the hell would we want to do that?

ANNIE. Because we have to. But be warned, once awakened the evil will conduct a ceremonial war ritual to honour the Necronomicon.

ASH. A ceremonial war ritual from hell...not looking forward to that. That's going to be hellish...guaranteed.

ANNIE. After the ritual is complete, recitation of the second passage will create a kind of rift in time and space that we will try and force the evil back through. But Ash, if anything happens to go awry during the reading of these passages, we have to be prepared…That's why you'll need this.

(ANNIE *hands him the chainsaw. He attaches it to his stump to a triumphant fanfare.*)

ASH. Groovy!

ANNIE. Okay…here goes. "Nos veratos alamemnon conda."

(*The cabin becomes dark as all of the previous characters return in their demon form [including* SCOTT, *who is not only now evil, but somehow the leader of the* DEMONS *as well]*).

SCOTT. Conda….Conda….

SONG: DO THE NECRONOMICON

CHERYL.

NOW WE HONOR THE NECRONOMICON

CHERYL, LINDA.

NOW WE HONOR THE NECRONOMICON

CHERYL, LINDA, ED.

NOW WE HONOR THE NECRONOMICON

CHERYL, LINDA, ED, JAKE.

NOW WE HONOR THE NECRONOMICON

SCOTT.

NOW WE HONOR THE NECRONOMICON WITH OUR
VERY OWN SPECIAL DANCE

ASH. *(spoken)* How the hell do demons do their very own special dance?

SCOTT.

IN HELL WE DANCE OUR OWN SPECIAL WAY
LETS SHOW 'EM HOW WE DANCE WHILE OUR BODIES
DECAY

LINDA.

DO WE BOUNCE LIKE BACKSTREET?

SCOTT.

NOT WITHOUT A HEARTBEAT

JAKE.

DO WE GRIND LIKE MICHAEL BIVINS?

SCOTT.

BEL BIV DEVOE BE FOR THE LIVING.

CHERYL.

DO WE WHOOMP LIKE TAG TEAM?

SCOTT.

NOT WITHOUT A BLOODSTREAM

ED.

LET'S MACARENA LIKE THAT GROUP DID.

SCOTT.

NO – THAT'S JUST STUPID

DEMONS.

DEADITES ALWAYS LIKE TO GET THEIR FREAK ON
AND WHEN WE GET TOGETHER WE DO THE
    NECRONOMICON
DO THE NECRONOMICON
DO THE NECRONOMICON
COME ON COME ON AND DO THE NECRONOMICON

SCOTT.

YOU GOTTA FOLLOW THE MOVES RIGHT TO THE
    LETTER
IT'S JUST LIKE THE TIME WARP
ONLY BETTER

DEMONS.

FIRST WE JUMP
THEN WE SINK DOWN
THEN WE GET BACK UP
AND LASSO ALL AROUND

THEN WE SPIN
CLAP OUR HANDS

DEMONS. *(cont.)*

> AND TAKE A BRIEF MOMENT
> TO ACKNOWLEDGE THE BAND

> DO THE ROBOT
> AND THE SPRINKLER
> AND FINISH IT OFF WITH
> OUR BEST HENRY WINKLER (AAAY)

> DEADITES ALWAYS LIKE TO GET THEIR FREAK ON
> AND WHEN WE GET TOGETHER WE DO THE
>   NECRONOMICON
> DO THE NECRONOMICON
> DO THE NECRONOMICON
> COME ON COME ON AND DO THE NECRONOMICON

LINDA.

> CAN WE KILL THESE SUCKAS YET?

SCOTT.

> JUST WAIT A LITTLE BIT

JAKE.

> CAN WE BEAT 'EM WITH A SHOE?

SCOTT.

> NOT TIL WE'RE DONE THE TUNE

CHERYL.

> CAN WE MUTILATE THESE FOOLS?

SCOTT.

> NO, FOLLOW THE RULES

ED.

> I SAY WE ATTACK

SCOTT.

> WHAT ARE YOU, ON CRACK?
> AFTER OUR DANCE WE'LL ATTACK OUR OLD FRIENDS
> BUT BEFORE WE DO THAT LET'S NECRONOMICON
>   AGAIN

DEMONS.

> FIRST WE JUMP
> THEN WE SINK DOWN

DEMONS. *(cont.)*

> THEN WE GET BACK UP
> AND LASSO ALL AROUND
>
> THEN WE SPIN
> CLAP OUR HANDS
> AND TAKE A BRIEF MOMENT
> TO ACKNOWLEDGE THE BAND
>
> DO THE ROBOT
> AND THE SPRINKLER
> AND FINISH IT OFF WITH
> OUR BEST HENRY WINKLER (AAAY)
>
> DEADITES ALWAYS LIKE TO GET THEIR FREAK ON
> AND WHEN WE GET TOGETHER WE DO THE
>   NECRONOMICON
> DO THE NECRONOMICON
> DO THE NECRONOMICON

ASH. How do we stop this horrible dance? I can't take another bad Henry Winkler impersonation. *(to* **DEMONS***)* That's your BEST Henry Winkler?

ANNIE. I only completed the first of the passages and that was to make the evil a thing of the flesh! They're dancing now, but soon they'll attack and take over all of mankind.

ASH. Then finish it! Quick!

ANNIE. There's still the second passage. The one to open the rift and send the evil back!

ASH. Well start reciting it! Now! Finish the passages! Get rid of it!

ANNIE. Conda nostrat– AHHHHHHH!

(The severed hand stabs **ANNIE** *with the dagger.)*

ASH. No!!! My hand again. Damn you hand.

ANNIE. I'm dying Ash.

ASH. No Annie, don't die. I can't destroy this evil without you.

ANNIE. You can Ash. You can. It's time for you to stand on your own. It's time for you to fight. It's time...

(**ANNIE** *dies in his arms.*)

SONG: IT'S TIME

ASH.

IT'S TIME,
TO FULFILL MY PURPOSE
IN LIFE
WE ARE BORN WITH A DESTINY

IT'S TIME
TO ACCEPT MY CALLING
TO GO
ON A RAVENOUS DEMON KILLING SPREE!

IT'S TIME TO FINALLY TAKE A STAND
FIGHT WITH MY STUMP AND MY GOOD HAND
STOP TALKING TRASH
AND KICK SOME DEMON ASS
IT IS TIME

SCOTT. *(spoken)* Oh its time Ash, but not for what you think...

DEMONS.

IT'S TIME FOR YOU, ASH TO DIE
IT'S TIME FOR US, ZOMBIES TO RISE
IT'S TIME FOR YOU TO SAY GOODBYE
IT TIME FOR....

ASH.

OH, IT'S TIME
TIME TO HURT DEMON FEELINGS
INSIDE
THESE HERE WALLS, THERE CAN BE ONLY ONE

IT'S TIME
TO INCREASE DEMON BLEEDING
TONIGHT
YOU WILL DIE BY THE SAW OR THE GUN

ASH. *(cont.)*

> TIME TO HARASS
> TIME TO WHOOP SOME ASS
> TIME TO KILL DEMONS EN MASSE
> OH IT'S TIME

DEMONS.

> TIME TO FIGHT.
> TIME TO BRAWL
> TIME TO KILL.
> TIME TO MAUL.
> KICK YOU SQUARE IN THE BALLS.
>
> IT'S TIME TO RIP YOU TO TATTERS
> TIME TO MAKE YOUR BLOOD SPLATTER
> THROUGH THE SHED
> JOIN THE EVIL DEAD
> IT IS TIME

ASH.

> YOU KNOW THAT I'M RIGHT!
> I'M NOT DYING TONIGHT, IT'S A HOLIDAY!
> WHEN I'M IN DESPAIR
> I ADJUST MY HAIR AND MAKE EVIL PAY
> AT THE EDGE OF THE NIGHT,
> THERE'S NOT A DEADITE I CAN'T HANDLE!

DEMONS.

> HANDLE!

ASH.

> WHEN DANGER CALLS,
> YOU MUST HAVE THE BALLS OF AN OX, OR A BEAR, OR
>   ANY LARGE MAMMAL!

DEMONS.

> ANY LARGE MAMMAL! YEAH!!
>
> IT'S TIME FOR YOU, ASH TO DIE
> IT'S TIME FOR US, ZOMBIES TO RISE
> IT'S TIME FOR YOU TO SAY GOODBYE
> IT TIME FOR…OH, IT'S TIME

ASH.

> IS THAT SO?
> I THINK NO!
> ALRIGHT, LET'S GO!
> OH, IT'S TIME!!!
>
> (**ASH** goes on the attack, individually killing each of
> the **DEMONS** in a variety of methods, each bloodier
> than the last. There's so much blood in this fight it
> even shoots onto the audience.)
>
> (After **ASH** has killed them all, he is triumphant...
> until suddenly, all of the **DEMONS** who **ASH** just
> killed come back to life.)

ASH. What? It can't be. You're coming back to life? No.
I killed you. I killed you all. You're dead.

> **SONG: WE WILL NEVER DIE**

DEMONS.

> YOU MUST REALIZE
> WE WILL NEVER DIE
> WE'RE ALREADY DEAD
>
> WE'VE DIED TWICE BEFORE
> BUT WE'RE BACK FOR MORE
> YOU CAN'T STOP THE DEAD
>
> YOU CAN'T KILL THE KILLED AND YOU CAN'T PASS ON
>   THE PASSED
> NOW WE'LL TAKE THAT CHAINSAW AND WE'LL SHOVE
>   IT UP YOUR...

ANNIE. (springing to life) ASH!!!!!

> (**ANNIE**'s scream brings the music to a screeching
> halt.)

ASH. Annie, you've sprung back to life. Seems to be
happening a lot around here lately. Finish reciting the passages Annie. Send these demons back
to hell!

ANNIE. Conda Conda Nosperoto ...DEMONTO!!!!!

(**ANNIE** *dies. But her reading of the passages successfully opens the rift in time and space, and all of the* **DEMONS** *get sucked through the cabin door.*)

ASH. You did it kid. You did it!!!! Annie! *(realizing she's dead)* Annie! Annie! No!!!!

(blackout)

Scene Eight

ASH. *(V.O.)* So with her dying breath, Annie read the passages, sent the Candarian demons back to hell, and together we finally put a stop to this unspeakable evil.

(The curtain opens to reveal ASH is now at S-Mart surrounded by random CUSTOMERS [the previous actors in bad wigs and mustaches].)

ASH. And that, loyal S-Mart customers is how I saved all of mankind.

MAN 1 (JAKE). And after saving all of mankind you came directly to work here at S-Mart?

ASH. No, I didn't come directly to work here at S-Mart. There was a brief period where I was sent back to Medieval Times and the people worshiped me as their king...but that's another story.

WOMAN 1 (LINDA). Wait, if Annie died in the middle of reading the passages, are you sure she said all the necessary words to dispel the evil correctly?

ASH. Well maybe she didn't say every single tiny little syllable, no. But basically she said them yeah... basically.

MAN 2 (SCOTT). Well all I can say is...wow...that story... is the biggest crock of shit I've ever heard in my life.

(They all start cracking up.)

MAN 3 (ED). I come here to buy some carpet and rug shampoo and I gotta listen to this crap.

MAN 1 (JAKE). I say we ignore this asshole and get back to our savings.

CUSTOMERS. Yeah.

(The CUSTOMERS go back to their shopping. WOMAN 1 (LINDA) approaches ASH)

WOMAN 1 (LINDA). You know that story about how you saving the earth from demons?

ASH. Yeah?

WOMAN 1 (LINDA). I…ah…think it's kinda cute.

ASH. Oh yeah?

(horn hits)

(A random customer in the background, **POS-SESSED WOMAN (ANNIE)** *turns around and is a demon.)*

POSSESSED WOMAN (ANNIE). Look who's evil now!

MAN 2 (SCOTT). Holy fuck!

(The **CUSTOMERS** *freak out.)*

*(***ASH** *grabs a gun off the shelf [still with the price tag hanging from it] and shoots it in the air.)*

ASH. Lady, I'm afraid I'm gonna have to ask you to leave the store.

POSSESSED WOMAN (ANNIE). Who the hell are you?

ASH. Name's Ash…housewares.

POSSESSED WOMAN (ANNIE). I'll swallow your soul.

ASH. Come get some.

*(***ASH** *shoots the* **POSSESSED WOMAN** *three times, killing her, and sending her flying offstage.)*

ASH. So do you screwheads believe I can save you from Candarian demons now?

(At this time, the actress playing the **POSSESSED WOMAN (ANNIE)** *will change her wig and outfit as fast as she can. Whenever possible, she will return to the stage mid-song as a completely different (non-evil) random customer for the big final number…)*

SONG: BLEW THAT BITCH AWAY

SCOTT.

WELL WE THOUGHT THAT YOU WERE FUCKING WITH
US

JAKE.

WE THOUGHT YOU WERE A LYING PRICK

CHERYL.

ALL THAT JIVE ABOUT YOU KILLING DEMONS

ED.

IT JUST SOUNDED LIKE BULLSHIT

SCOTT.

BUT APPARENTLY YOU WEREN'T TALKING SMACK

CHERYL.

CAUSE WE SAW THAT EVIL CHICK

LINDA.

SHE WAS GOING TO EAT US

JAKE.

AND SEVERELY BEAT US

SCOTT.

TIL YOU SHOT HER IN THE TITS

JAKE.

THAT'S RIGHT YOU SAVED US

CUSTOMERS.

YOU SAVED OUR LIVES

CHERYL.

YOU SAVED ME, AND MY BABY AND THESE GINSU
KNIVES

CUSTOMERS.

YOU SAVED US ALL

ED.

YOU'RE THE BADDEST MOTHERFUCKER IN THIS
WHOLE STRIP MALL

CUSTOMERS.

WE THOUGHT YOU WERE A PHONY ON SOME MAD
TIRADE

CUSTOMERS. *(cont.)*

> BUT NOW WE SEE THAT YOU'RE A HERO AND YOU
> > SAVED THE DAY
>
> BECAUSE YOU BLEW THAT BITCH AWAY ASH!

ASH.

> WELL I TOLD YOU I COULD KILL THESE DEMONS
> AND NONE OF YOU BELIEVED ME

CUSTOMERS.

> NO NO NO YEAH

ASH.

> THAT'S WHY YOU'RE MERELY CUSTOMERS
> WHILE I'M THE S-MART EMPLOYEE

CUSTOMERS.

> YEAH YEAH YEAH OH YEAH

ASH.

> CAUSE I KILL WHAT LOOKS EVEN SLIGHTLY EVIL
> WHO KNOWS WHO THE NEXT VICTIM WILL BE

CUSTOMERS.

> NOT ME

ASH.

> CAUSE I SHOOT

CUSTOMERS.

> SHOOT

ASH.

> AND KILL

CUSTOMERS.

> KILL

ASH.

> AND SAW

CUSTOMERS.

> UNTIL

ASH.

> WE NEED A CLEANUP ON AISLE THREE

CUSTOMERS.

> YOU ARE THE MAN

ASH.

I BITCH SLAP EVIL WITH MY ONE GOOD HAND

CUSTOMERS.

YOU'RE OUR HERO

ASH.

I SHAKE DOWN DEADITES LIKE THEY OWE ME DOUGH

I SAW THAT DEMON TRYING TO RUIN YOUR SHOPPING
DAY

CUSTOMERS.

SHOPPING DAY

ASH.

SO I GRABBED MY TWELVE GAUGE AND I BLEW HER
AWAY

CUSTOMERS.

BLEW THAT BITCH AWAY

JAKE.

THAT'S RIGHT YOU BLEW

CUSTOMERS.

BLEW THAT BITCH AWAY

JAKE.

YOU BLEW THAT BITCH AWAY

CUSTOMERS.

BLEW THAT BITCH AWAY

JAKE.

YOU BLEW HER TO SMITHEREENS

CUSTOMERS.

BLEW THAT BITCH AWAY

JAKE.

YOU BLEW HER LIKE A DRUNK TEEN

CUSTOMERS.

BLEW THAT BITCH AWAY

CUSTOMERS & JAKE.

BLEW THAT BITCH AWAY

WE USED TO FUCKIN' HATE YOU AND YOUR LYING
WAYS

BUT NOW WE'VE CHANGED OUR MINDS AND THINK
YOU'RE OKAY

(As everyone sings, **ASH** *rips off his S-Mart uniform
revealing the outfit he has been wearing all show.
He puts the chainsaw on his stub.)*

CUSTOMERS.

BECAUSE YOU BLEW THAT BITCH AWAY
BLEW THAT BITCH AWAY
YEAH!

(ASH *grabs* **WOMAN 1 (LINDA)** *and passionately
kisses her as the lights go down)*

The End

OTHER TITLES AVAILABLE FROM SAMUEL FRENCH

SCREAM QUEENS

Scott Martin

Musical Comedy / 6f (ages 28 - 50+)

"They sing – they dance – they die!"

A hotel ballroom, 1998, and six voluptuous B-movie "Scream Queens" revive their fading acting careers by presenting a musical revue for their fans at a science fiction and horror film convention. From young newbie to seasoned grand dame, the Queens strut their stuff in song and dance to prove "I Got All of the Talent I Need." For 90 minutes of hilarious musical mayhem, they take the audience into the world of no-budget movies with awful scripts, fake monsters and gooey "Special FX." They even involve the audience in a screaming contest and zombie talent search.

As each Queen reveals her personal story, we share their hopes and dreams, from Tonya's love of her idol "Fay Wray" to Alexis' advice that "Everybody Starts at the Bottom" to DeeDee's secrets of Scream Queen longevity: "Don't Open That Door." British screen veteran Nadine savors her joy of being "Still In Demand" while Bianca celebrates the lifetime achievements of "Roger Corman" and Richelle laments her own elusive "Happy Endings." They also screen original clips from their direct-to-video "scary movie" spoofs such as "Revenge of the Psycho Bimbos" and "Malibu Vampire Vixens," all hoping to attract the attention of a popular young horror film director lurking in the audience.

The Scream Queens will have you convulsed with laughter and begging for the inevitable sequel.

"A sassy musical revue; an affectionate funny tribute…with something for everyone."
–*Los Angeles Times*

"Campy and full of shtick, affection and great fun!"
–*The Hollywood Reporter*

SAMUELFRENCH.COM

SLASHER

Allison Moore

Comedy / 2m, 4f

When she's cast as the "last girl" in a low-budget slasher flick, Sheena thinks it's the big break she's been waiting for. But news of the movie unleashes her malingering mother's thwarted feminist rage, and Mom is prepared to do anything to stop filming...even if it kills her.

The hilarious hit of 2009's Humana Festival of New American Plays at the Actors Theater of Louisville.

"Screaming. Blood. Impalements. Meat hooks. Electric drills. Objectified sexy women. Crazy mother in wheelchair. Whaddya expect? It's a slasher movie."
– *Philadelphia Inquirer*

"*Slasher* elicits laughs by intentionally indulging in everything that makes horror films atrociously unentertaining."
– *Broad Street Review*

"Moore manages to bring a plethora of contemporary themes into the play, from feminism to militant pro-life groups to an insider's view of the horror-movie genre...It's a job well done!"
– *San Francisco Examiner*

OTHER TITLES AVAILABLE FROM SAMUEL FRENCH

NEIGHBORHOOD 3: REQUISITION OF DOOM

Jannifer Haley

Dark Comedy / 2m, 2f, expandable casting up to 7m, 8f / Unit Set

In a suburban subdivision with identical houses, parents find their teenagers addicted to an online horror video game. The game setting? A subdivision with identical houses. The goal? Smash through an army of zombies to escape the neighborhood for good. But as the line blurs between virtual and reality, both parents and players realize that fear has a life of its own.

"Playing like a nifty episode of *The Twilight Zone*, the story builds to an affectingly gruesome finale…with its small-scale tech demands and four-person ensemble, *Neighborhood* seems a likely candidate for legit troupes hoping to benefit from the play's youthful, tech-savvy appeal."
– *Variety Magazine*

"When our player pounds on the video door, and we hear the bang on his own front door, it's genuinely, brilliantly chilling."
– *Denver Post*

"Haley's suspenseful play beamed cautionary messages about inattentive parents of teenagers addicted to online video games. A sense of unease about the diminishing line between real life and virtual reality lingered for days after the suburban zombies in *Neighborhood 3* were vanquished with weed whackers and hedge clippers."
– *Louisville Courier-Journal*

OTHER TITLES AVAILABLE FROM SAMUEL FRENCH

ADDING MACHINE: A MUSICAL

Composed by Joshua Schmidt
Libretto by Jason Loewith and Joshua Schmidt
Based on the play *The Adding Machine* by Elmer Rice

Comedy / 3m, 2f and SATB chorus / Unit Set

WINNER! 2008 Lucille Lortel Award - Outstanding Musical

WINNER! 2008 Outer Critics Circle Award - Outstanding New Off-Broadway Musical and Outstanding New Score

Darkly comic and heartbreakingly beautiful, *Adding Machine*, a musical adaptation of Elmer Rice's incendiary 1923 play, tells the story of Mr. Zero, who after 25 years of service to his company is replaced by a mechanical adding machine. In a vengeful rage, he murders his boss. An eclectic score gives passionate and memorable voice to this stylish and stylized show, which follows Zero's journey to the afterlife in the Elysian Fields where he is met with one last chance for romance and redemption.

"Exciting and adventurous!"
– NY Post

"**** THE BEST NEW MUSICAL of 2008!"
– Time Out New York

"A BRILLIANT MUSICAL! A superb libretto by Loewith and Schmidt and music that gets under your skin and stays there."
– New York Times, Critics Pick

"A MARVEL! Joshua Schmidt's music sneaks up on us until we are begging for more! *Adding Machine* dazzles!"
– Bloomberg.com

"A MASTERPIECE of expressionism. Brave and bold!"
– Variety